JET AGE

The Comet, the 707,

and the Race to Shrink the World

Sam Howe Verhovek

AVERY

a member of

Penguin Group (USA) Inc.

AVERY

Published by the Penguin Group
Penguin Group (USA) Inc., 375 Hudson Street, New York, New York 10014, USA •
Penguin Group (Canada), 90 Eglinton Avenue East, Suite 700, Toronto, Ontario M4P 2Y3, Canada
(a division of Pearson Penguin Canada Inc.) • Penguin Books Ltd, 80 Strand, London WC2R 0RL,
England • Penguin Ireland, 25 St Stephen's Green, Dublin 2, Ireland (a division of Penguin Books Ltd) •
Penguin Group (Australia), 250 Camberwell Road, Camberwell, Victoria 3124, Australia (a division of
Pearson Australia Group Pty Ltd) • Penguin Books India Pvt Ltd, 11 Community Centre, Panchsheel
Park, New Delhi–110 017, India • Penguin Group (NZ), 67 Apollo Drive, Rosedale, North Shore 0632,
New Zealand (a division of Pearson New Zealand Ltd) • Penguin Books (South Africa) (Pty) Ltd,
24 Sturdee Avenue, Rosebank, Johannesburg 2196, South Africa

Penguin Books Ltd, Registered Offices: 80 Strand, London WC2R 0RL, England

Photographs: *p. xiii:* United Airlines Creative Services; *pp. 1, 149* (top): © BAE SYSTEMS; *pp. 23, 81, 111, 211:*
The Boeing Company Collection at The Museum of Flight; *pp. 37, 149* (bottom): Science Museum / SSPL;
p. 179 (left) © Boeing; (right) British Airways Heritage Centre

Most Avery books are available at special quantity discounts for bulk purchase for sales
promotions, premiums, fund-raising, and educational needs. Special books or book excerpts
also can be created to fit specific needs. For details, write Penguin Group (USA) Inc. Special
Markets, 375 Hudson Street, New York, NY 10014.

Library of Congress Cataloging-in-Publication Data

Verhovek, Sam Howe.
Jet age : the Comet, the 707, and the race to shrink the world / Sam Howe Verhovek.
p.   cm.
Includes bibliographical references and index.
ISBN 978-1-58333-402-7
1. Aeronautics, Commercial—History.   2. Jet planes—History.   I. Title.
TL515.V37   2010   2010023848
629.133'349—dc22

Printed in the United States of America
1   3   5   7   9   10   8   6   4   2

Book design by Susan Walsh

While the author has made every effort to provide accurate telephone numbers and Internet addresses at the
time of publication, neither the publisher nor the author assumes any responsibility for errors, or for changes
that occur after publication. Further, the publisher does not have any control over and does not assume any
responsibility for author or third-party websites or their content.

Lisa, come fly with me

CONTENTS

It is doubtful if aeroplanes will ever cross the ocean. . . .
The public has greatly over-estimated the possibilities of the
aeroplane, imagining that in another generation they will be able
to fly over to London in a day. This is manifestly impossible.

*—William Pickering,
astronomer, Harvard University, 1908*

From the commercial point of view, I see no prospect of large
aeroplanes, carrying large numbers of passengers, competing
either in price, convenience, safety or even in speed, with trains.

*—Mervyn J. P. O'Gorman,
Superintendent, His Majesty's Balloon Factory (UK), 1911*

In the opinion of competent experts it is idle to look for a
commercial future for the flying machine. There is, and always
will be, a limit to its carrying capacity which will prohibit its
employment for passenger or freight purposes in a wholesale or
general way. There are some, of course, who will argue that
because a machine will carry two people another may be
constructed that will carry a dozen, but those who make this
contention do not understand the theory of weight sustentation
in the air.

—W. J. Jackman and Thomas Russell,
Flying Machines: Construction and Operation, *1912*

They'll never build 'em any bigger!

*—C. N. "Monty" Monteith,
chief engineer, Boeing Airplane Company,
on introduction of the ten-passenger Boeing 247, 1933*

JET AGE

Preface

This is a book about the first generation of jet airliners and the people who designed, built, and flew them. Long before there was a World Wide Web, the jet airplane wove the world together by enabling people to travel great distances in a matter of hours, and thus must rank very high on the list of humanity's most important technological creations. If medieval serfs or the Founding Fathers were somehow transported forward in time to the present day, what would they find most astonishing? Google Earth, perhaps. The iPhone, sure, though I suspect that before too long they would rib us about all the dropped calls. But I think there's a good chance that they would be most amazed by our jetliners, whizzing around up there at more than 500 miles per hour.

The dream of flight goes back to the very beginning, when man first saw bird, but it is only in the last few generations that it has been fulfilled. Yet today the modern airliner is in so many ways a victim of its own success, such a commonplace that few of us even pause to look at one soaring in the sky or think much about jet travel at all except when it inconveniences us, when our plane is crammed to the gills with all those other people or delayed by hours as we inch forward on a taxiway, waiting for all those other planes to take off or land.

It was once terrifically exciting to travel on a jet airliner. That is in stark contrast to today, when the European jet-building consortium mundanely calls itself Airbus, and indeed most people think of air transport as a "glorified bus operation," in the words of Michael O'Leary, the chief executive of the European low-cost carrier Ryanair. Actually, one could quibble with the "glorified" part.

Airliners once had lounges; today, we are warned not to congregate in too big a line for the bathroom. It is safe to say that air travel no longer inspires most of us to sartorial heights, but people once got dressed up in their finest clothes to step aboard a jet plane, and both airplane manufacturers and the airlines did a conscious and effective job of selling jet travel as something chic, glamorous, romantic, elegant, exciting, sexy, magic. Even the great U.S. poet and historian Carl Sandburg struggled a bit to capture the thrill of the first commercial jet flight from New York to Los Angeles, in 1959, on which he was a passenger.

"You search for words to describe the speed of this flight," Sandburg wrote soon afterward. "You are whisked and streaked, you are zipped and flicked, you are sped, hurtled, flashed, shuttled from an ocean on one side of the continent to an ocean on the opposite side in less time than it takes the sun to trace a 90-degree arc across the sky."

The path to the Jet Age was triumphal and, in the grand scheme of things, amazingly rapid—less than fifty years after the Wright brothers' first flight at Kitty Hawk, Great Britain led the world with the first commercial jet, the de Havilland Comet. But Manifest Destiny in the air was laced with tragedy, most notably in the deadly and mysterious flaw of this pioneering airliner, which caused three Comet jets to blow apart in the sky, killing everyone aboard.

The story culminates in the October 1958 race between two airplanes—and between two nations, two global airlines, and two rival teams of brilliant engineers—for bragging rights to the first jet service across the Atlantic Ocean. This Anglo–American competition came right down to the wire at New York's Idlewild Airport (today's JFK), pitting the Comet, flown by the British Overseas Airways Corporation and completely redesigned to correct its fatal flaw, against the Boeing 707, launched into its inaugural service by Pan American World Airways.

The horse race in the sky had only one winner, but in a larger context, the aviation industry itself was now poised for an era of dominance. Until 1958, more people crossed the Atlantic Ocean aboard ships than on airplanes, and in the United States, the ten largest transportation companies that year were all railroads. Fewer than one in ten American adults had ever even been on an airplane.

The jet airplane changed everything, not just consigning many ships to the cruise industry and trains to the freight yards, but exponentially increasing the number of overall passengers among nations. The modern-day Magellans who designed and flew it really did shrink the world, in the sense that they changed our perceptions of distance in relation to time.

Cities that were once six days apart became six hours apart; the idea, in the mind's eye, of "how far" it was from New York to Los Angeles changed, from four days to five hours, in less than a generation.

Before jet travel, only the very wealthy could afford—in sense of the time or the money—to cross back and forth over the oceans. True, a much larger number of immigrants crossed the Atlantic and the Pacific in ships to get to the United States, but those who did so knew that when they left their birthplaces, they would most likely never set eyes on the old country again. Today, even people of relatively modest means—a Filipina nurse working in Kuwait, the Punjabi taxi driver taking you home from the airport in the United States—are able to return by jet to see loved ones once a year.

Jet airplanes gave us a wider range of choices of the heart, as people on opposite coasts or even in different nations found they could carry on "long-distance relationships" in a way simply not imaginable to any other generation in history. They opened vast new possibilities for mass tourism, such as sunny beach escapes in the middle of winter. Hawaii, for example, had just 171,367 visitors in 1958, the year before Pan Am introduced jet service to Honolulu; within five years of that inaugural flight, this annual tourism figure had tripled, and by 1970 it was 1.75 million. Today it's 7 million, with virtually everyone going in and out on a jet airplane.

Jetliners have been essential to the growth of Internet commerce, enabling companies like Amazon.com to deliver us just about any product overnight and making FedEx so busy moving all those boxes around that at one point it began dispatching five empty jets to roam the skies every evening, waiting for orders on which city needed help with the overflow. Jets sped globalization; they gave a name to an entire well-heeled globe-trotting class— the "jet set"—and to a new, mind-warping physical condition— "jet lag." They also guaranteed that dangerous viruses could be spread across the globe in a matter of hours.

One man had a particular influence on the way we fly today: Bill Allen, the Boeing president who pushed his board of directors to bet the company on both the 707 and, later, the 747. A securities lawyer and widower thrust into the president's role quite unexpectedly and with zero engineering background, Allen was a placid guy who looked like the archetype of the 1950s corporate "man in the gray flannel suit," the industry equivalent of the bald, plodding Dwight D. Eisenhower. Far more ink has been spilled on the aviation titan whose airline was the launch customer for both of these jet airplanes, the mercurial Juan Trippe of Pan American World Airways. The two men reached a deal on the 747 while on a fishing trip in Alaska in the mid-1960s. "If you build it, I'll buy it," Trippe told Allen, who replied: "If you buy it, I'll build it." He did and he did, and the era of the jumbo jet came to pass.

At the time, Pan Am was the world's largest and most important international airline, and its demise—given its leading role in bringing air travel to a much broader swath of humanity— was all but unthinkable. Why, the company had its own skyscraper in midtown Manhattan (the largest office building in the world when it opened in March 1963), from the top of which customers could catch a helicopter to meet their Pan Am plane at the airport. It had partnered with another giant company, IBM, to build PANAMAC, a revolutionary teleprocessing system launched in 1964 that enabled thousands of travel agents around the world to secure nearly instant reservations on Pan Am flights for their clients—a splendid and very cool innovation, long before the Internet allowed us to compare hundreds of flights and fares with a single key click. Pan American was the lead customer in line with fifteen orders for the Boeing 2707, a supersonic transport that was to be America's answer to the European Concorde. Along with the red Coca-Cola label, the blue Pan Am globe was among the most universally recognized symbols of American industry. In perhaps the iconic Pan Am photograph, four young men stepped off a Pan American 707 jet from London at New York's John F. Kennedy International Airport one day in 1964, waving to the crowd that greeted them at the bottom of the moving stairway. The Beatles had arrived.

The downfall of Pan Am—along with the deaths of other airline behemoths such as Trans World, Braniff, Eastern, and Western—makes for a powerful business fable, reminding us that while we debate whether Microsoft or Google will run the computing world, either or even both could be out of business in a generation. But while Trippe would have vividly captured Shakespeare's imagination as a character, I bet the bard would have also noted that boring old Bill Allen was doing something right. Allen took over a company that was a three-time loser in the commercial airliner business, with less than 1 percent of the market share in 1950, and under his watch it became the most dominant and creative airplane builder in the world, eventually driving the onetime U.S. giants—Douglas and Lockheed—out of the jetliner industry altogether. So, while Allen hardly cut the mold as a dashing or daring figure, and the most titillating detail in his personal diaries was an annual resolution to cut back on the cocktails, I hope this book will give him some due as a visionary and a business leader.

To me, one remarkable facet of Boeing's story is how right they got it the first time around. Fifty years later, we are not flying any faster or in any greater comfort than was the case when Pan Am flew its first 707.

Moreover, airlines are no longer battling with one another to cut down our waiting times to board. It's not their fault, of course: security is paramount, and screening takes time. Still, it's hard not to envy the air traveler of half a century ago on this account. As a July 1959 article in *Time* magazine detailed it, Continental Airlines was even selling the tickets aloft on its new Boeing 707 flights between Chicago and Los Angeles. "Passengers will be able to arrive at the airport up to ten minutes before flight time," the article explained, "versus the usual 20 or 30 minutes now required by most lines."

Supersonic air travel has come and gone, and by all accounts will take quite a while to come back again, if it ever does. In truth, some of the most intriguing proposals for hyperspeed travel across the oceans involve neutrally buoyant tunnels through the sea and magnetically levitated trains, not aircraft, which could theoretically link the city centers of New York and London in an hour.

The computer, of course, has changed radically in the past half-century. The jet airplane has not. The only real difference, though it's a huge one, is that we are flying around far more cheaply than we could in 1958, and in vastly larger numbers. By the mid-1970s, half of all U.S. adults had flown, and today the figure is nearly 9 in 10. We complain about crowded airplanes and poor service, but the situation reflects that most travelers, as the saying goes, have three criteria in mind when choosing an airline: price, price and price.

Still, for all the hassles involved in jet travel, it is worth pausing every once in a while to marvel at the ingenuity of the modern airliner and to appreciate just how far we have come. As we shall see, the jetliner represented a radical improvement over an earlier generation of propeller-driven airplanes that shook, sickened, and even broke the bones of passengers in the 1930s. "When the day was over my bones ached, and my whole nervous system was wearied from the noise, the constant droning of the propellers, and exhaust," one airline customer recalled of such a flight.

When Boeing's chief test pilot, Tex Johnston, flew a Boeing 707 jet prototype with a planeload of reporters from Seattle to Baltimore in three hours, forty-eight minutes, one day in March 1957, it was duly noted that he had set a new transcontinental speed record. "We knew darn well that we were participating in a giant step forward in the evolution of the airplane," recalled William Randolph Hearst, Jr., the newspaper publisher. But in addition to the feeling of tremendous power and speed, Hearst and others on the press junket seemed even more impressed with something else. "The outstanding difference," Hearst said, "was in its total lack of vibration. This we proved to ourselves by balancing pencils and cigarettes and even standing coins on edge on the tables."

We are at the threshold of an interesting new era of air travel today, which in some ways carries echoes of the great British–American competition of the 1950s. Boeing's chief rival is now Airbus, the European consortium, and both manufacturers have bold next-generation jetliners with which to attract the attention of the world's airlines—and their passengers.

Intriguingly, despite the stereotypes, it is the Europeans who have gone for the Super Size: the A380, a posh double-decked, four-engine whale of an airplane that is capable of seating nearly forty times as many people as the venerable DC-3. Boeing has focused on the smaller, evocatively named 787 "Dreamliner," a two-engine carbon-composite long-distance aircraft that promises a greater sense of roominess, bigger windows, quieter, more fuel-efficient engines, and better air quality compared with its predecessors'. But while these new airplanes vie to be the next big thing in air travel, neither offers the quantum leap in speed and comfort that the first jetliners did over their propeller precursors.

The first jet airliners were, simply, wondrous machines. For all the justifiable awe at how the World Wide Web has revolutionized our lives and connected human beings around the globe, the jet airplane gave us worldwide wings. It is undeniably the machine that has connected our world in the most real, tangible of ways, truly linking more people in more places than any other invention in history. This is the story of how we got there.

one

The de Havilland Comet

Porto Azzurro, Italy
January 10, 1954

The first jet airliner ever to fly soared homeward bound toward London now, on the final leg of a journey that had started in Singapore and included stops in Bangkok, Rangoon, Karachi, Bahrain, Beirut, and Rome. The jetliner was called the Comet, and it was somehow elegant and understated at the same time. It appeared almost impossibly sleek, its four "Ghost" engines tucked into the wings, not far from the cabin, so that to someone watching it blaze across the sky, the Comet seemed almost like a paper airplane: it was hard to see *what* was actually propelling it. The jet Comet flew nearly twice as fast and twice as high as any aircraft in the generation of propeller-driven passenger planes that preceded it in flight. Unlike those prop planes, the Comet could sail above most bumpy pockets of the atmosphere, up to a serene spot where the planet itself started to fall away; why, any higher, and one could see the curvature of the earth.

The artistic design of the Comet's livery was all British reserve: white and silver with a thin line of royal blue running along the row of squared windows, just four letters painted on each side: BOAC. But this design was so modest, really, that it was immodest, for most everyone knew that the de Havilland Comet, the new flagship of the British Overseas Airways Corporation, was actually a symbol of astonishing ambition. Staggered and exhausted in the postwar years, its earthly empire unraveling from the Far East to India to Africa to the Caribbean, Great Britain was nonetheless out to create a new domain: an empire in the sky.

As airlines and aircraft makers elsewhere in the world had held off on developing jet airliners, with concerns ranging from technical feasibility to safety to the frightful expense of it all, the postwar British government had made a giant bet in the other direction and poured smarts, sweat, and sterling into building the jet Comet. British leaders were certainly not operating under any illusion that they could rule the world anymore, not in the emerging global struggle between the United States and the Soviet Union. The sun, which once never set on the British Empire, now rose on a Cold War world. But if the British no longer had the most powerful nation on earth, they could still be the most technologically dazzling and the most scientifically advanced. They no longer ruled the waves, but now they might reign in the air.

This idea of British prowess, this aspiration, was reflected not only in the jet airplane program, but in British popular culture as well. After all, the ultimate character in the field of "intelligence," the world's wittiest and most unflappable secret agent, was a British operative by the name of Bond, James Bond. Less globally enduring but still hugely popular in the postwar United

Kingdom was another fictional British character: Dan Dare, "Pilot of the Future," a science-fiction comic-strip figure who stood atop the field of intergalactic adventure just as Bond outwitted every other spy in the known universe.

Colonel Daniel MacGregor Dare of the Interplanet Spacefleet emerged in 1950 on the pages of a British boys' magazine, and Bond in 1953 in the English author Ian Fleming's debut novel, *Casino Royale*. And between the appearance of these imaginary heroes, in 1952, the futuristic de Havilland Comet started flying passengers—tangible, nonfictional evidence that Great Britain could indeed develop world-beating technology. Lest anyone miss the point, BOAC said in its inaugural announcement that the new passenger jet would fly Empire Service routes to some of the most distant points in the no-longer-actual empire. It was this very airliner (not just the model, the very airplane) that had kicked off the whole venture on May 2, 1952, on a flight that took off promptly as 30,000 spectators in and around London Airport (today's Heathrow) cheered her on.

"And so to Khartoum, silvery in the waning moonlight," a British reporter said of the maiden flight as it sped toward Africa. Next, "the brazen sun tipping the rim of the desert as the Comet winged southward to Entebbe." Another stop for fuel "in the midday furnace heat of Livingstone." And finally, some twenty-three and a half hours and 6,774 miles later, the British Overseas Airways Corporation's de Havilland Comet landed at Johannesburg's Palmietfontein Airport before a jubilant crowd of 23,000. It was two minutes ahead of schedule. *The Times* of London was exultant over the pioneering flight by the craft with its "shining silver wings" and small blue speed-bird image on the tail. "This distinction, shared by a British operator and a British product," the newspaper proclaimed, "set the seal on this country's lead in applying the gas turbine to civil aviation." Other Comets soon came off the de Havilland factory line in Hatfield, England, and cut cleanly across the skies like fish through water, bound for Australia, India, Japan. The Comet was a spectacle everywhere it went, its takeoffs and landings watched by throngs that in some cities were allowed to gather right along the very edges of the runways—dazzled spectators with picnics and cameras, and fingers pointing to the sky. "The British are proud of the Comet," noted Clifton Daniel, the London bureau chief of *The New York Times*, adding that the aircraft had "put them years ahead of the rest of the world in jet transport and restored their confidence in their inventiveness."

It was a big status symbol to be aboard the BOAC's bullet-shaped jet Comet, ensconced in seats covered with a blue herringbone-weave wool-faced tapestry, streaking through the stratosphere at 500 miles per hour and seven miles above the earth. The cabin held just thirty-six passengers—with the fuel-guzzling engines, de Havilland's engineers simply couldn't make the plane any bigger at that point. There was a mini-library just next to the entrance foyer, separate bathrooms for men and women, an ashtray at every seat, even a special Comet cocktail served only aboard the jetliner—three-sixths brandy, two-sixths fresh-squeezed grapefruit juice (yellow, not pink), one-sixth Van Der Hum liqueur, a dash of Angostura bitters, and a sliver of lemon peel. Tickets for many flights sold out months in advance.

Surprisingly, neither of the two emerging superpowers had a jet airliner yet. This was a springboard to private diatribe in the Soviet Union, where Premier Nikita Khrushchev angrily ordered his top engineers and the Aeroflot apparatchiks to step it up, and to public fulmination in the United States, where politicians and the press had suddenly demanded to know how the most powerful nation on earth could lack a jetliner with which to dazzle the world.

"Whether we like it or not, the British are giving the U.S. a drubbing in jet transport," fumed the editor of *American Aviation* magazine, Wayne Parrish. "The bald truth is that the British are forcing the U.S. to take up the challenge—or lose both air traffic on important world routes and sales in important world markets."

Juan Trippe, head of Pan American World Airways, the dominant U.S. international air carrier, wasn't going to wait for American air manufacturers to get their act together. Trippe, immensely suave and single-minded in his determination to make Pan Am the world's leading airline, had used his acumen and his clout in Congress to gain monopoly control among U.S. carriers over service to dozens of foreign destinations.

Pan Am may have been launched in 1928 with an overly grandiose name, derived from its single hundred-mile mail-carrying route between Key West, Florida, and Havana. But now the "World" was more operative than the "Pan American," for the company had become a truly global hegemon. Launching round-the-world service in 1947, Trippe liked to boast that his goal was nothing less than to shrink the world.

True enough, the shrinking involved more than one hundred hours and stops in Honolulu, Wake Island, Guam, Tokyo, Shanghai, Hong Kong, Bangkok, Calcutta, Karachi, Damascus, Istanbul, London, and Shannon, Ireland, at a cost of about $21,900 in today's dollars. But Trippe, with ambitions so vast that economic historian Matthew Josephson dubbed him the Emperor of the Air, had a plan to slash those times and those ticket prices—with jetliners.

In the autumn of 1952, Trippe had stunned both the airline and aircraft industries by announcing orders for three British-made Comets, with an option for seven more. It was the first time any major American carrier had ever ordered a foreign-made aircraft. Eddie Rickenbacker, the garrulous World War I U.S. flying ace and the head of Eastern Air Lines, made an even more audacious announcement. He would pay $100 million for thirty-five Comet jets. There was a catch: he wanted every last one of them by 1956, a proviso that would force de Havilland to both ramp up production and slip Eastern ahead of some European airlines that had already placed orders. "If I were an Englishman," cracked Rickenbacker, "I would work day and night, including weekends, to keep the advantage they have."

For U.S. manufacturers, all of this amounted to an obvious and humiliating slap in itself, but just to drive home the point, Pan Am's chief engineer, André Priester, sent out a holiday card in December 1952 to every aircraft builder and airline in the United States. It depicted the Old North Church in Boston with a jet flying overhead, and three lanterns in the church's famous tower. Not one if by land or two if by sea, but now three, because it was by air. "The British Are Coming!" screamed Priester's holiday greeting.

The British were so confident in the Comet that just weeks after the maiden commercial flight, the Queen Mother and Princess Margaret took a four-hour sightseeing jaunt "at royal request" over continental Europe in a Comet. The airplane was commanded by Group Captain John "Cat's Eyes" Cunningham, de Havilland's chief test pilot and a World War II hero whose night-fighting prowess was so great that he forever carried a vivid nickname that he, in fact, disliked. The moniker arose largely from a wartime propaganda profile of him that carefully excised all details of major advances in Britain's night-radar capabilities and instead claimed his pilot's eyes were so good because he ate huge amounts of carrots. (He did not.)

The royal party aboard the Comet looked down on France, Switzerland, Italy, and Corsica—and Cunningham even let the Queen Mother briefly take the controls. On landing at Hatfield, the Queen Mother sent a telegram to the RAF's 600 Squadron in London, of which she was the honorary commodore. "I am delighted to tell you that today I took over as first pilot of a Comet aeroplane," wrote the fifty-one-year-old Queen Mother. "We exceeded a reading of 0.8 Mach at 40,000 feet. What the passengers thought, I really wouldn't like to say."

BOAC's chairman, Sir Miles Thomas, announced that faster, bigger, longer-range British-built jetliners were already in the works, and in a speech in Canada the normally reserved Sir Miles even gave way to a touch of hubris. He pronounced the British character "strangely attuned to this air age," just as it had been to another era—when Great Britain ruled the waves.

"To work in fluid elements, between ugly danger and calm transcending beauty, as are the sea and the air, brings out the best in a Britisher," the chairman told the Empire Club of Canada, in Toronto, in October 1953. "This present Elizabethan age is repeating in the air what the first Elizabethan era saw at sea."

In a way, national pride in the Comet was only magnified by the austerity and drabness of postwar British life, of a London that was "now the largest, saddest and dirtiest of great cities," as the English writer Cyril Connolly put it, "with its miles of unpainted, half-inhabited houses, its chopless chop-houses, its beerless pubs, its once vivid quarters losing all personality, its squares bereft of elegance." Eight years after the end of the war, rationing was still in effect for sweets, meat, and bacon.

Nonetheless, things *were* looking up. *Fortune*, the American business magazine, conceded that 1953 was "the year of the Coronation and the Comet." *Time* called the Comet "the new queen of the airways." Not only did the UK have the world's fastest airplane, it was triumphing in other ways as well. A British-backed expedition led by Sir Edmund Hillary of New Zealand reached the highest point on earth, the summit of Mount Everest, in May 1953, and planted the Union Jack. At Oxford, a twenty-four-year-old English medical student named Roger Bannister was quietly training for a singular goal: to be the first man in the history of the world to run a mile in less than four minutes. And in London, the government was promising that the coming year would bring "Derationing Day," the end of all restrictions on food sales. With Elizabeth II atop the throne, Bannister pacing himself at ever-faster intervals, and yet more Comets streaking across the sky, 1954 looked to be a promising year for the British as well.

And so on this second Sunday morning in the new year, the de Havilland Comet had roared down the runway at Rome's Ciampino Airport and soon sliced through heavy clouds. No one on the ground could see it, but anyone who could hear the high, loud grinding whine overhead—its four jet engines "screaming like tortured banshees," as one magazine writer put it—knew exactly what it was. Aboard BOAC Flight 781 was a polyglot collection of passengers, representative of the former Empire: children from diplomatic families headed from Pakistan and Burma to London for the new semester at boarding school, businessmen in oil and publishing, and a famed World War II correspondent, Chester Wilmot, an Australian who had covered it all—the futile prewar diplomacy, the major battles, the trials at Nuremberg—and written a definitive account, *The Struggle for Europe*. Frank L. Saunders, the flight's steward, and Jean Evelyn Clark, the stewardess, prepared for a tea service. The twenty-three-year-old Clark was a last-minute substitute at Rome that morning, standing in for a female colleague who had fallen ill with the flu and thus couldn't make the final leg of the flight.

Captain Alan Gibson, who had won the Distinguished Flying Cross for his mastery of bombers during the war, pointed the great flying machine northwest toward London. The Comet climbed through 26,000 feet in airspace over the Italian island of Elba, where Napoleon was exiled in 1814. The Comet overtook a London-bound BOAC Argonaut, a propeller-driven plane whose captain, J. R. Johnson, later recalled that Captain Gibson had "promised to give me the top of the cloud"—in other words, to relay word of the altitude at which his ship had reached the clear blue sky. Captain Gibson did so and followed up a few minutes later with a radio transmission to the lower, slower plane.

"George How Jig from George Yoke Peter," said Gibson, crisply using the UK pilots' phonetic alphabet for the call letters of each airplane. "Did you get my . . ." The transmission cut off abruptly as the de Havilland Comet blew apart in the sky, instantly killing everyone on board.

Leopoldo Lorenzini, a truck driver on Elba, heard a series of quick explosions, and then a great crescendo of roaring noise. He craned his neck toward the gray sky and there saw "a red flame falling into the sea, followed by a trail of smoke like a spiral." Nearby, Ninuccio Geri, a sailor, also heard "a heavy roar, like thunder." He turned and saw "a globe of fire rotating as it came down into the sea." Giovanni di Marco, a fisherman, saw "a silver thing flash out of the clouds." A fourth man, Vasco Nomellini, a farmer out on a seaside hill near a Napoleonic-era military fort, cast his gaze at the leaden sky but reported seeing something more distinct: "Two pieces of an aircraft, the smaller in flames, falling in almost parallel lines into the sea."

It was just past eleven o'clock in the morning. Most in the Mediterranean fishing village of Porto Azzurro were at Mass;

a few were sipping glasses of Carpano in the square. Quickly, an alarm was relayed across Elba, and a small flotilla of fishing boats was rounded up. A local harbormaster, Colonel Giuseppe Lombardi, a compact, robust man dressed in an overcoat several sizes too big, was led aboard a small motorboat and took command of the search.

The men of the village pointed the boats in the direction of the balls of fire they had seen hit the sea. It was only an hour or so before they encountered slicks of kerosene. Soon the searchers were casting down their nets to haul in the first flotsam of a disaster: Cushions. A smart blue dress. An Oriental cigarette case. A child's stuffed bear. A ripped postal sack.

By now, the crackle of Lombardi's radio had brought news from the Italian military command. BOAC's Comet, with twenty-nine passengers and six crew, had disappeared. Scour the sea for any possible survivors.

In Hertfordshire, England, a telephone rang, and a shy, gaunt man who had been relaxing in his study with the Sunday papers took the call. The news was brief. "Sir, the Comet has gone in." The man who took this news was Sir Geoffrey de Havilland, age seventy-one, the leading pioneer and legend in British aviation.

In 1909, de Havilland built and flew his first airplane with the help of his new wife, Louise, a former governess to his younger sisters, who stitched the canvas wings with a hand sewing machine. It crashed. He survived. He built a stronger one. He built an even better one, and the British government bought it, the first of literally dozens of airplanes that would bear the distinctive D.H. designation.

In 1928 he and Louie (the name by which everyone knew his wife) broke the world altitude record of 21,000 feet in a de Havilland Moth, a small straight-winged biplane. He was a supreme airplane designer, though one often unable to express his ideas in precise engineering terms. "I like a thing to look right," he once explained. "If it does not, although I may not be able to prove it wrong scientifically, I have often found out later that it is."

De Havilland's obsession with flight and speed was both genetic and tragic. Two of his three sons had died in test flights with de Havilland aircraft—John, in 1943, during a midair collision in a war-training exercise, and Geoffrey Jr., in 1946, in a tailless, experimental jet that was trying to break the sonic barrier over Egypt Bay near the village of Allhallows-on-Sea, England. The younger Geoffrey was flying faster than any man had ever flown before when his plane broke apart. Louie, the young men's mother, suffered a nervous breakdown and died in 1949, officially of cancer but "more likely from a broken heart," as Sir Geoffrey later put it. Sir Geoffrey turned the stiff upper lip, and carried on. He married a woman he met on safari in Kenya, and doted on his first cousins in Hollywood, Olivia de Havilland (of *Gone With the Wind* fame—she was Melanie) and Joan Fontaine. And in 1952 he unveiled to the world his most magnificent aeronautical accomplishment yet: the DH-106, known as the Comet.

For de Havilland, the disastrous news from Italy was not, in fact, the first problem for the Comet. A year to the day after the triumphal maiden passenger flight, a BOAC Comet had broken apart just six and a half minutes after takeoff from Calcutta's Dum Dum Airport, killing all forty-three people aboard. British and Indian authorities concluded the plane had been taken down by a freakishly vicious thunderstorm. Two other Comets had been seriously damaged in incidents involving pilots struggling with a sudden, unexpected rolling of the plane just after takeoff.

For all of these problems in just a year and a half, however, no one among the senior members of the British aviation establishment would blame the airplane itself. "The Comet's all right," Sir Miles, head of the government-backed BOAC, told reporters in a bit of English concision a few weeks after the Elba incident. The royal air authority announced there was "no justification for placing special restrictions on the Comet aircraft." Sabotage—a theory flagged by newspapers across the slowly unwinding Empire—was a prime suspect in the Comet explosion over Elba. Perhaps the Burmese or the Pakistanis, the Lebanese or the Italians, were not sufficiently vigilant to stop a bomb from being placed aboard the jet. Security was stepped up at all stopover points.

As for the other incidents? Pilot error was suggested by aviation experts as the possible explanation. Not everyone agreed. Gerhard Nitschke, former chief test pilot for the German jet pioneer Heinkel, put it most bluntly: "Something is wrong with this bird. What, however, I do not know." In any event, after just a few weeks of inspection following the Elba disaster, all seven of the remaining Comets in the BOAC fleet were put back into service.

The flying public itself seemed to put a vote of confidence in the Comet, with the jet booked on average to more than 90 percent of its capacity. Sir Miles, the BOAC chief, made a point of flying on the plane to demonstrate his faith in it, and in his 1964 autobiography, which carried the slightly disconcerting title *Out on a Wing*, he recalled interviewing several of the passengers who had boarded the jetliner despite its worrisome safety record.

"The general reaction was, 'Well, if it's good enough for the captain and crew, it's good enough for me,'" wrote Sir Miles. "But there was one lady who, when I asked, 'Why did you book this particular service?' said, 'I absolutely loathe flying and this one seems to get there the quickest, so that's why I'm going on it.'"

On April 8, 1954, another Comet was boarding at Rome's Ciampino Airport, this one bound for Cairo. "This is progress," proclaimed one of three Americans who boarded, Ray Wilkinson, a shoe-parts manufacturer from Massachusetts. "Sure, they've had accidents, but everything is OK now."

Once again a Comet jetliner roared down the runway at Rome, this time heading south for Egypt. As it rose in the evening sky, one passenger began to compose a letter to his sweetheart. "My darling: the blue Mediterranean Sea is under us and the coast appears in the distance as a dark shadow," he wrote. "In the sky there is much light, and never as now have I been so happy."

A few minutes later, he was dead.

Incredibly, just sixteen days after reentering service, another de Havilland Comet simply blew apart in the sky, this one plunging in pieces into the Tyrrhenian Sea; yet again, all on board were killed. "Crash" was simply not the right word to describe this latest disaster, or the ones over India and off Elba that preceded it. Each of these airplanes somehow experienced sudden, explosive decompression. One second the Comet was gliding through the sky, its passengers perhaps enjoying a cup of tea, or a cigarette, or both. The next second the plane broke apart, killing all passengers and crew immediately by bursting their lungs. Authorities announced a reexamination of the Comet that had been destroyed in the Indian thunderstorm. Could it be sabotage in all three cases? Possible, but extremely unlikely. The more likely terrible truth was that the pioneering Comet had a fatal, mysterious flaw.

In time, the tragic failure of the de Havilland Comet would prove to be as grievous a blow to British pride as the sinking of the *Titanic* in the North Atlantic in April 1912. Curiously, though, the loss of confidence in the aircraft developed slowly, over a period of months and only after this series of disastrous explosions, followed by a massive inquiry that finally offered the definitive explanation of the cause. Conversely, in a time when the world moved more slowly, the horror of what was wrong with the Titanic was flashed almost instantly around the world: the great ship declared unsinkable had obviously been sunk, by an iceberg.

After the third Comet explosion, authorities finally took the decisive step. All remaining Comets were grounded, and the prime minister, seventy-nine-year-old Winston Churchill, returned to power after a narrow Tory victory a few years before, announced:

"The cost of solving the Comet mystery must be reckoned neither in money nor in manpower."

Because the Comet destroyed in the January disaster was in significantly shallower waters than those that swallowed up her sister craft in April, it was this plane that would become the centerpiece of a remarkable salvage effort by the British Navy, and of one of the biggest, most expensive, and most complicated pieces of industrial detective work ever attempted.

Word went out to Admiral Lord Louis Mountbatten, commander-in-chief of the Mediterranean fleet in Malta: "Endeavour to locate and salve crashed Comet." Over the next several months, naval search teams painstakingly recovered nearly 70 percent of the doomed airplane, transporting the thousands of pieces to the Royal Aircraft Establishment at Farnborough, the nerve center of British aviation, where it was reassembled like a jigsaw puzzle around a giant scaffold. Sir Geoffrey and Sir Miles soon turned their attention to solving the Comet case. But to do so, they needed a master detective. The man they tapped was a brilliant scientist and mathematician named Arnold Hall, a six-foot-tall, thin, angular professor of aviation who puffed on a pipe continuously and who had a gift for explaining complicated things in clear layman's terms. As one British author put it, Hall was "practical, precise and can reduce all scientific phenomena to simple language, understandable to most men, even politicians and journalists."

Churchill implored Hall to leave no stone unturned in examining the great riddle. Hall agreed: "Let's have a jolly good go," he said, "with nothing in the way."

Hall placed a Comet airplane in a giant water tank and subjected it to countless pressurization tests; built human-sized rubber dummies and had them dropped from planes thousands of feet above the ground, to study just how the Comet's victims died; subjected one hundred wooden models of the Comet to every conceivable act of turbulence, stress, and violence; and even flew with members of his staff in some fifty airborne tests of yet another Comet plane, a manifestly dangerous undertaking but one that Hall deemed essential to cracking the case.

"They were going as close to the tiger as possible," explained Sir Lionel Heald, a Crown representative in the inquiry, "hoping it would not get them."

If Hall could figure out the Comet's fatal flaw, there was still a chance the problem could be fixed and the redesigned Comet could reemerge as the flagship of the world's major airlines. If not, then the Comet's name would indeed prove tragically apt— it would be an airplane that blazed an amazing bright trail across the skies, but then quickly flared out.

Perhaps even more fundamentally, Hall's inquiry might be able to answer some of the questions being asked nearly everywhere, from pubs around London to the pages of newspapers around the world. Was the Comet flown too soon? Had British air authorities, in a rush to lead the world into the Jet Age, taken a reckless gamble with human lives?

To some, given the scope and repeat nature of the disasters, the answers were evident: yes and yes. Some seemed willing to reserve judgment until the inquiry could reveal just who knew what, and when. And yet, to many others, the definitive and certainly most dramatic answer ultimately came not from Professor Hall, but from another titan of British aviation whose testimony at the inquiry proved mesmerizing.

This was the legendary Lord Brabazon of Tara, a pioneering pilot who held the very first official pilot's license in the Kingdom (B-1) and who had headed the panel that, a decade before, committed the nation to building the jet Comet.

Rising to speak before the court of inquiry, Lord Brabazon thundered: "You know, and I know, the cause of this accident. It is due to the adventurous, pioneering spirit of our race. It has been like that in the past, it is like that in the present, and I hope it will be in the future."

In words that some considered the essence of British drive and daring but others thought a grave affront to mourning relatives of all those killed aboard the Comets, Brabazon continued: "Here is a great imaginative project, to build a machine with twice the speed and twice the height of any existing machine in the world. We all went into it with our eyes wide open. We were conscious of the dangers that were lurking in the unknown. We did not know what fate was going to hold out for us in the future.

"Of course we gave hostages to fate," continued Lord Brabazon, "but I cannot believe that this Court, or our country, will censure us because we have ventured. You would not have the aeronautical people in this country trail behind the world in craven fear lest they be censured in such a Court as this for trying to lead the world. Everything within the realm of human knowledge and wisdom was put into this machine."

But that was all to come long after this sad January day, when fishermen urged on by the rumpled, tireless harbormaster continued their grim task under the overcast sky. At four-twenty, just over five hours after the crash, the men on the trawler *Francesco Giuseppe* gently raised the first of the dead from the sea. It was a boy, no more than ten or eleven years old. Next to be laid on the makeshift morgue on the deck was Jean Clark, the twenty-three-year-old stewardess who had come aboard at the last moment to replace her flu-bound colleague.

In all, thirteen more bodies were pulled from the Mediterranean in the next hour and a half, until dusk began to fall. This meant that more than half of the passengers remained unaccounted for, but the condition of those who had been found left no doubt in anyone's mind that there were possibly any still alive. A surgeon who examined them later noted a striking consistency in the faces of the dead: "They showed no look of terror," he said. "Death must have come without warning."

Shortly after six p.m., the fishing boats sailed back for Porto Azzurro in the gathering darkness. There the fishermen carefully placed the bodies on wooden planks, covered them with clean white sheets, and carried them to rest overnight in the local chapel. They lit candles, and most everyone in the village gathered to say prayers for the dead.

two

The Boeing 707 Jet Stratoliner

Seattle, Washington
August 7, 1955

In the Seattle of 1955, there was no Space Needle yet, no iconic, futuristic structure to give the city a signature skyline. Tucked away in that quiet upper left-hand corner of the map, Seattle was seven years away from hosting the World's Fair, and twelve years from gaining its first major-league sports team. Yet Seattle had something to show the world, and in recent months the eye and ear had been drawn upward toward it—a large, loud fast-moving blur of metal soaring over the waters of Puget Sound and above the Cascade and Olympic mountain ranges. This 95-ton silver, brown, and canary-yellow bird was the prototype for a passenger jet being developed by the local aircraft company. That firm happened to have been located in Seattle nearly forty years before on the whim of a young Michigan lumber and mining magnate and Ivy League dropout.

William Edward Boeing—his German father was named Wilhelm Böing, the son wound up with an Anglicized version of the name, and told most everyone to call him Bill—had come to the Pacific Northwest just after the turn of the century to check out the timber prospects. They were fine, indeed, and Bill Boeing settled in Hoquiam, a tough little logging town near the Pacific coast in southwestern Washington state.

This wealthy, strapping, and energetic young man became much wealthier, buying and selling timber tracts, and before too long he was spending most of his time in Seattle, itself a somewhat rough-around-the-edges port town, but a decidedly more upscale place than Hoquiam. And when his fancy was seized by flight during his very first trip aloft, aboard a hydroplane over Seattle's Lake Washington on the Fourth of July, 1914, it did not take long for Bill Boeing to imagine himself as an aircraft maker. He respected the skills of the pilot, Terah Maroney, but he did not think so highly of the pilot's boxy, drafty stick-and-wire Curtis floatplane, he told a friend who also flew that day, G. Conrad Westervelt, a naval lieutenant and engineer. Then Bill Boeing made a rather brass assertion.

"You know, Westervelt," he said, "there isn't much to that machine of Maroney's. I think we could build a better one!"

The two men's B&W Seaplane, made of wood, wire, and Irish linen, with a 125-horsepower engine and a top speed of 75 miles per hour, was in the air by June 1916. Westervelt was called back East for naval duty, and soon the company was all Boeing's. Though the market for airplanes was much larger on the other side of the country, Boeing decided to stick it out in Seattle chiefly for this reason: there was so much good *wood* in the area. "Built Where the Spruce Grows" was the Boeing Airplane Company's motto. As time went by, aluminum replaced wood as the preferred material for aircraft, and as it happened, the Pacific Northwest was an ideal place for this commodity, too. Cheap hydropower from the Columbia and other great rivers of the region powered the plants that produced all the aluminum. The phenomenal efforts of Boeing and other aircraft manufacturers helped lead the Allies to victory in World War II. But as the 1950s dawned and the Korean War sputtered down into a stand-off, the Boeing Airplane Company had a giant challenge on its hand, one that company executives sometimes delicately referred to as "the peace problem." While Boeing had thrived as a military manufacturer, its performance in the commercial market bordered on the anemic. It suffered from something of a Goldilocks syndrome: some of its civilian planes wound up too small for the passenger market, and some too big.

In 1933, the Boeing company had introduced what, at that time, was a stunningly modern airplane, the 160-mile-per-hour ten-passenger, twin-engine Boeing 247, the first airliner with all-metal construction, deicing equipment, and retractable landing gear. The cabin ceiling was just under six feet high.

But Boeing's innovative airliner quickly turned into an also-ran to a legendary airplane built by the Southern California–based Douglas Aircraft Company. The Douglas engineers had countered the 247 with the fourteen-passenger DC-2, soon followed by the twenty-one-passenger DC-3. The civilian DC-3 and its military counterpart, the C-47, together made for one of the most successful and distinctive airplanes of all time, with more than 13,000 built, flown by airlines around the world and still in use today, for everything from cargo trips around Alaska to aid missions in Africa. In 1939, a single model of airplane, the DC-3, carried 90 percent of the world's airline passengers.

Powered by two large propeller engines, the DC-3 had two large tires under the front of its fuselage and a single, smaller one in back. It was ungainly but strangely compelling in takeoff. As the DC-3 lumbered down a runway, it tilted upward in such a way that it was abruptly rolling on its front wheels, looking for all the world like it might tip over on its snout. With a bit more speed, however improbably, it jumped off the runway and headed for the clouds.

Douglas Aircraft seemed to have a magic touch as it developed new, bigger propeller planes into the 1950s: the DC-4, the DC-6, the DC-7 (nicknamed "The Seven Seas"). However bumpy the ride, however many refueling stops needed to get there, these were the planes used by most of the world's carriers to transport passengers across the country or across the oceans. Meanwhile, Lockheed Aircraft was working in concert with Trans World Airlines' principal owner, Howard Hughes, who even with spells of madness was one of the most visionary figures in aviation history. Together they came up with the elegant Lockheed Constellation, nicknamed the Connie, a dolphin-shaped, triple-tailed, four-engine airplane that in some configurations was the most luxurious machine ever to soar in the sky. Some had eighteen sleeper cabins, with crisp linen sheets and turndown service, and featured fresh flowers and four-course meals.

Boeing, by contrast, was a three-time loser in the commercial aviation industry. Not only was the 247 a slow seller, but the company also lost millions on the big, bulbous-nosed Flying Clipper airships operated by Pan American World Airways in the late 1930s, and it lagged with the luxurious but expensive "Stratocruiser," a giant flying tub of a plane that was vastly out-sold by its Douglas and Lockheed competitors.

As the 1950s began, Seattle-based Boeing had less than 1 per-cent of the commercial aircraft market, and even that share was eroding, for Boeing did not even have a single new commercial airliner in the design stage. But in a way, Boeing's failures con-tained promising seeds of fortune—for the company made a move initially eschewed by its more successful competitors in civil aviation. Boeing decided to build a jet airliner.

Boeing's decision represented an astounding gamble and, for five lonely years, the company forged ahead without even per-suading a *single customer* to commit to buying its airplane, in either its commercial or military configurations. Some of the best and brightest luminaries in the airline industry questioned whether there was much need or demand for jet-speed travel. "We can't go backward to the jet," said C. R. Smith, president of American Airlines, announcing a large order for more of the prop-driven DC-7s that were already raking in plenty of money for both Douglas and American. Ralph Damon, president of Trans World Airlines, said simple economics favored a $1.5 mil-lion propliner such as the Constellation over the $4 million jet being peddled by Boeing, even if the latter offered a faster and less bumpy ride to the passenger. "The only thing wrong with the jet planes of today," said the head of TWA, "is that they won't make any money."

So Boeing built a single prototype, officially called the 367-80 but much more widely known by the company nickname "Dash-80," and this was the plane that had started showing up in the skies over the Puget Sound region in 1954.

The airplane would become known as the 707, a machine whose DNA can be deduced in any Boeing jetliner designed and flown since. It was perhaps not as recklessly beautiful as the British Comet. Rather than sleekly hiding the engines by building them into the wing roots, the Dash-80's jets hung down somewhat ungainly from the wings on spindly struts. This was a more practical if less elegant placement, allowing easier maintenance and even a quick replacement if needed. It would prove safer. The windows were rounded—not as crisp as the straight lines that made up the squared windows on the Comet, whose designers wanted them that way to distinguish their airplane's windows from the porthole windows of a ship. That insistence would prove costly, in so many ways.

More than anything, though, the Dash-80 was big. In fact, it could hold nearly three times as many passengers as the original Comet, and even the company's top officials conceded the plane was so much bigger than any before it that a single crash could instantly become the most deadly accident in the history of aviation, perhaps even the death knell for the whole enterprise. "It was a question of policy as to whether you should expose one hundred people to the hazards of commercial aviation, and whether Boeing could survive the headlines of a hundred people being killed in a single crash," recalled one senior executive, Maynard Pennell.

Moreover, Boeing, after fishing around with zero success among the nation's major airlines to find a paying partner in the development of its jetliner, took an audacious step when it decided to build the plane on its own. The board committed $15 million—a huge figure for the day, representing a quarter of the firm's net worth—for research and development of what it simply called "Project X." It did so largely at the prodding of one man—William McPherson Allen, the company president.

Self-effacing, introspective, a balding, jug-eared lawyer raised in small-town Montana, Allen hardly fit the mold of a swashbuckling gambler. The airline world was full of such larger-than-life characters—Trippe of Pan Am; Hughes of TWA; Rickenbacker of Eastern, which dominated lucrative routes linking the Northeast with Florida vacation spots and the rest of the South.

Bill Allen was not a pilot. He was not an engineer. He recalled no childlike fascination with flight—and, in any event, airplanes were certainly not a major sight in the Big Sky country in the early 1900s, when he was growing up in the Bitterroot Valley community of Lolo, selling cherries from the family orchard. He was conservative by nature, in his politics and, at first, with his approach to Boeing's finances. But Bill Allen, in his own quiet way, wound up as the biggest gambler of all. Twice he would push the Boeing board of directors to bet the company on a single commercial airplane—the 707 in the early 1950s and the 747 in the late 1960s, a financing and development strain that could easily push it to the brink of bankruptcy.

It was Bill Allen who sat on a boat this sunny August day in 1955 with old friends, relaxing and awaiting the start of Seattle's famed hydroplane Gold Cup races on Lake Washington. He was one of 350,000 people gathered in or around the lake to watch the races, and among the crowd were hundreds of visitors who made up a veritable Who's Who of the world's aviation industry. For at this time, Seattle was the host to two major conventions—that of the International Air Transport Association, or IATA, an organization that regulated routes and fares of the world's international airlines, and of the Aircraft Industries Association, which represented the nation's leading aviation manufacturers. Word was leaked that Boeing's Dash-80 jet would do a test run during a break in the race schedule. For many in the air industry, it would be their very first look at the giant jet plane. There was still much skepticism about the economics of a jet—and concern about whether it was safe. After all, look what had happened with the British Comet—three frightful crashes, and the rest of the fleet still grounded.

The massive bird lumbered down the runway, south of downtown Seattle, and headed west out over the Olympic Peninsula for an initial round of tests. This was an airplane insured for $18 million, with one unusual provision in the contract. Only one man could be at the controls.

This man was Alvin M. "Tex" Johnston, the company's chief test pilot, who oozed all of the swagger that Allen, his boss, kept so carefully in check. Strong, profane, funny, he was a character practically out of Hollywood's central casting—in fact, he would serve as a model for the Slim Pickens bomber-pilot character in Stanley Kubrick's dark-comedy Cold War classic, *Dr. Strangelove*.

Johnston often insisted on wearing his cowboy boots and even his Stetson when he flew, and on the wall of his office at Boeing headquarters he hung a sign that, however humorously, let people know his view of his place in the pecking order of a company filled with brilliant designers and engineers.

"One test is worth a thousand expert opinions," the sign read.

Everybody called him Tex, though few knew the gag behind the name: he was actually from Kansas, and he'd acquired the nickname early in his career in Niagara Falls, New York, where he was testing fighter planes. Arriving at work one day in 1943 in his trademark Stetson and polished cowboy boots, Johnston got an approving nod from a mechanic, who said: "Get your 'chute, Tex. You get the first one today." The name stuck.

Johnston got his start as a barnstormer in his native state, where at one point he earned his keep as a daredevil with Inman's Flying Circus, for which he played the part of a drunken country bumpkin, flying crazy loops and zags with his Ford trimotor plane as nervous audiences craned their necks to watch the show and see whether he'd crash. Occasionally he'd do a complete roll of the airplane.

At Boeing, the chief pilot irritated the engineers by cussing if he didn't like their drawings. He was a font of corny sayings: nobody died, in Tex Johnston's world, he just "departed from the earth-bound flight pattern." And he could be crude. The Tex Johnston of this era wouldn't make it through the first three minutes of today's workplace-sensitivity training.

In a psychoanalyst's office in Seattle's Capitol Hill neighborhood in 1948, Tex Johnston was undergoing a mandatory preemployment mental-fitness evaluation. The female doctor interviewing him was tall, with "liquid brown eyes," complemented by "dark brunette hair and her full and enticing mouth," as Johnston cheerfully described it all a half-century or so later. He said he "played along" when she pulled out the standard peg set of the era, and complied by putting the round pegs in the round holes and the square pegs in the square holes. Then she asked a series of questions—Why are you a test pilot? Why did you choose Boeing?—winding up at: "What do you like better than anything in the world?"

"Copulation!" said Tex.

The interview was over. Apparently he passed, since Boeing hired him, though he was rejected when he asked the analyst for a date. "I'm new in Seattle, but I understand the Ben Franklin has a delightful restaurant, the Outrigger," said Tex as he stood up to leave. "Would you have dinner with me tonight?" The woman stared at him for a moment. "No-o-o," she drew out her answer. "I believe not." Johnston walked out with a tip of his cowboy hat, and said: "It was indeed a pleasure."

Tex Johnston's actual engineering instruction in the principles of aerodynamics was limited, but he was nonetheless recognized as a genius at flying, a sort of Michael Jordan among pilots, a man with a sixth—and seventh, and eighth—sense of what his airplane could do.

Tex, an admiring colleague once said, "could make anything fly."

Johnston was cruising on this Sunday afternoon at about 450 miles per hour in the Dash-80; he cut it back and came down over Lake Washington at only 300 feet. The audience oohed and aahed and pointed at the brightly colored jet. He pulled the big jet up at a 35-degree climb. And then the screaming plane dipped its wing and started to turn over, rotating slowly, at one point completely upside down, the yellow-and-silver tail section pointing straight down toward the water and the jet's huge underbelly facing upward toward the heavens.

On board his boat, Allen, the company president, briefly felt sick to his stomach. The 707 was his baby, and it looked to be soaring out of control. If it crashed anywhere near the crowd, it could cause hundreds of deaths. If it crashed anywhere, the 707 project would clearly be dead—and so would the company.

But then, as Allen and the rest of the crowd watched, the plane continued its roll until it had completed a full 360-degree rotation. The plane soared several hundred feet higher, then reversed course and came in again toward the lake—toward all the boats in the water, toward the huge crowds on shore.

Again, the Boeing 707 prototype tilted and went into a slow, full-circle rotation overhead. No one could hear Tex Johnston, of course, but up in the pilot's seat, he was letting out whoops of joy.

This time, Bill Allen did not feel sick. He managed to stammer out a joke to Larry Bell of Bell Aircraft, one of his guests on the boat. "Larry, give me about ten of those heart pills you've been taking," he said. "I need 'em worse than you do."

Inside, though, Bill Allen was no longer worried. Now he was seething. As soon as the boat got to shore, he called a meeting of his top executives for early the next morning at Boeing headquarters, and there was only one item on the agenda: what to do with Boeing's chief test pilot, Tex Johnston.

three

Dreamers and Aviators

William Henson's proposed "aerial steam carriage," 1843.

For I dipt into the future, far as human eye could see,
Saw the Vision of the world, and all the wonder that would be;

Saw the heavens fill with commerce, argosies of magic sails,
Pilots of the purple twilight dropping down with costly bales.

—*Alfred, Lord Tennyson, "Locksley Hall," 1842*

Early on the humid evening of July 25, 1944, a twin-engine propeller plane took off from the Royal Air Force base at Benson, in Oxfordshire, and headed southeast toward continental Europe. The airplane, a 1,460-horsepower de Havilland Mosquito, soon crossed into German airspace, and the two men on board began working methodically through a punch list. Though the Allies were at war with the Nazis, this Mosquito was unarmed: the men's job was not to shoot weapons, but to shoot photographs. On their aerial reconnaissance mission, they would snap images and bring back critical information for their commanders, intelligence to be scrutinized for evidence of Nazi troop movements and factory activities. The lack of weapons aboard was not a source of grave concern, for the de Havilland Mosquito could fly faster and maneuver more deftly than any aircraft the Luftwaffe had previously thrown at it. It had the lowest loss rate of any Allied aircraft in World War II.

But as the men reached 29,000 feet, roughly over Munich, RAF Flight Officer A. S. Lobban spotted something unusual at 4,000 yards astern: the outline of an aircraft closing quite rapidly toward him. No Allied aircraft was known to be in the area; this object fit no profile of a Nazi airplane ever seen by either Lobban or the chief pilot, A. E. Wall. As it drew closer, the strange aircraft became only more confounding. With a protruding bulletlike nose and a large underbelly, it looked almost like a shark. As it drew closer, both men could hear, above the rat-a-tat patter of their propellers, that this twin-engined machine made a very different kind of noise, something almost like a wailing scream.

As Lobban warned of the approaching craft, Wall responded by giving full power to the throttle. But the other craft quickly overtook the Mosquito, passing just overhead and to the right. It cut a swift arc to the left of the British plane. Wall cut sharply to the right, but the enemy machine quickly locked in pursuit. At 800 yards out, this new German aircraft opened fire.

With no ability to engage in a firefight, the pilot decided to turn in, quickly cutting down the enemy's angle of fire, almost like a boxer coming in close to clench his opponent, limiting the damage of a blow. He was almost on the German's tail when the Nazi aircraft broke away.

Three more times, the German pilot circled up and came back in for the attack, opening fire each time but not managing to land any hits on the smaller British plane. On the next pass after that, the screaming German airplane went into a shallow dive and then came directly up from below, cutting loose with another blast of fire. Wall turned sharply to the left and directed his craft upward as well; as he did so, both men later recalled, they heard two muffled explosions underneath them. Lobban, the flight officer, dropped down and quickly discovered that the outer hatch of the emergency exit had torn off at both hinges. Both men had parachutes and quickly agreed they would have to bail if the damage grew much worse.

As Wall prepared for a sixth round of attack from the enemy plane, he noticed some cumulous clouds below, at about 16,000 feet. He angled the plane sharply downward toward them and soon the men were diving through a cotton-ball blanket of whiteness. Three to four minutes later, the RAF Mosquito broke through the lowest layer of clouds and all was quiet. There was no trace of the enemy aircraft. Checking maps, they found an abandoned airstrip at Fermo, near Venice, and made an emergency landing.

The Jet Age, the RAF flyers reported to their superiors, was now officially under way.

Like many technologies, the jet engine was forged in the urgent crucible of war—when funds flow fast for a vital strategic objective, when engineers and builders work around the clock, and when authorities deem it in the national interest to order young men to take frightful risks with strange new machines, the kinds of risks that might never be sanctioned in a civilian setting. Thus it was with jet-powered airplanes. And for the Allies in the summer of 1944, for all the ways in which the tide of the war had seemed to turn inexorably in their favor, here was one area where they found themselves at an alarming disadvantage. The enemy was now producing the Messerschmitt Me 262, the world's first operational jet.

"This jet-propelled aeroplane is a feature in which we are definitely behind the Germans," Prime Minister Churchill bluntly summarized to his cabinet shortly after the Mosquito's encounter with the Nazi aircraft. He added this even more succinct order to his air chiefs: "Catch up as soon as possible."

An airplane moves because a powerful rush of air traveling in a backward direction propels the plane forward. In simplest terms, this principle of flight fascinates any child who blows up a balloon, lets it go, and watches it fly away. The escaping *whoosh* of air, the child's own self-created little jet stream, sends the balloon speeding in the opposite direction. In scientific terms, powered flight is in perfect accord with Newton's Third Law of motion: Every action has its own equal and opposite reaction. Push air behind you, and you can make an airplane zoom ahead, equally fast. Figure out a way to push air downward fast enough, and eventually you can rocket your way to the moon.

We understand these principles today and in retrospect, the ever-faster engine progression from propellers to jets to rockets over the last century or so seems obvious and inevitable. For most of recorded history, however, as we have considered what

French aviator Louis Blériot called "the most beautiful dream that has haunted the heart of man," human beings envisioned a very different sort of engine that might allow us to soar across the sky. This engine was man himself. We have envied the birds for as long as we have watched them fly, and wondered whether we could somehow do so ourselves.

In the greatest single bit of mythology surrounding flight, created by the ancient Greeks, man achieves the dream. Daedalus creates the wings that enable himself and his son, Icarus, to escape captivity. Hubris destroys the dream when the rapturous Icarus ignores his father's warnings and flies too close to the sun, melting the wax of his wings and plummeting him back to earth.

For many centuries, the power of the Icarus image held great sway. No less a scientist than Leonardo da Vinci believed that man could "sustain himself by the flapping of wings." The trick was to invent the right kind of wings with which to flap, and a disturbingly large number of volunteers, variously known as "birdmen" and "batmen" (in all recorded instances, they were indeed men, not women) killed or maimed themselves over the centuries in the attempt.

Alas for these dreamers in particular and for mankind in general, we were not meant to fly, at least in the sense of being able to beat our artificial wings and generate the power to take off, gain altitude, and soar and swoop. The human body is an amazing thing, but aerodynamically or physiologically suited for flight, it is not. There are a hundred reasons why, but perhaps the simplest is that we literally don't have the heart for it. The great beating heart of a hummingbird represents nearly one quarter of its total weight. In a golden eagle, the heart is about 8 percent; in man, it is about one half of 1 percent.

Strictly speaking, it is not impossible for man to engage in a kind of flight. We can jump out of airplanes and drop thousands of feet, preferably with a parachute, and we can ride the winds in gliders. In what is to my mind one of the more underappreciated feats of human physical accomplishment, a man has actually flown under his own power across the English Channel—on gossamer wings, poetically enough. On June 12, 1979, a 137-pound, superbly conditioned amateur bicyclist and fourth-generation Californian named Bryan Allen slipped the surly bonds of earth from a chalky cliff near Dover and began pedaling with all his might.

Allen was the sole power propelling a device named the Gossamer Albatross, constructed of superlightweight carbon fiber composite tubes, polystyrene ribs, and Mylar film. The aerial contraption weighed just over half of what he did but nonetheless had a thin white wingspan of ninety-six feet, wider than that of a DC-9's. Allen's used his hands to control and direct the wind-whipped Albatross, and his feet to pump away at pedals that drove a chain that turned a propeller that made the whole thing fly. In a nonstop fury of cycling, dipping at times to within inches of the water and driving himself to the brink of hallucinatory exhaustion, Allen stayed aloft for twenty-two miles and nearly three hours before touching down on the beach at the base of the Cape Gris Nez radar station in France. He and a team of designers thus claimed a $205,000 Royal Aeronautical

Society prize put up by a British industrialist. Allen went on to set other world distance and duration records pedaling a small blimp named the *White Dwarf*, and he holds on to a day job at the Jet Propulsion Laboratory in Pasadena, California, working as a software engineer in the Mars exploration division.

Allen is a freak, a sort of aerial version of Lance Armstrong. As remarkable as his flight was, the cycling-propelled aircraft does not represent a practical way for the rest of us to fly around, no matter how hard we work out at the gym. And despite the centuries of images of wings, golden chariots in the sky, flying sticks, and magic carpets, the fact is that for most of human history, nobody really had a clue how to design an aircraft—more specifically, a vehicle with the motor and the wings that could help a man lift off the ground, achieve significant altitude, and descend to a safe landing.

Brave aeronauts did start going aloft toward the end of the eighteenth century, during a largely France-centric craze for hot-air ballooning. Jean-Pierre Blanchard, who became a national hero for his feats, soared to 12,500 feet in a hydrogen balloon in 1784, and the next year he ballooned across the English Channel. Somehow Blanchard managed to stay on the good side of the French monarchy, the French Revolutionists, and Napoleon, generating respect and goodwill for the French across Europe. He did the same in the new United States of America, where in 1793 he conducted the first manned balloon flight in North America, an event witnessed by President George Washington as well as future presidents John Adams, Thomas Jefferson, James Madison, and James Monroe. Blanchard happily ballooned away until age seventy-five, when he suffered a heart attack during a demonstration over The Hague in 1809, fell out of his balloon, and died.

As exciting and colorful as hot-air balloons were and still are, they remain subject to the winds, and have never represented a reliable or economically feasible way to get from one place to another. As steam-engine technology rapidly improved during the 1800s, some believed this might at last be the way to power an aircraft. One especially imaginative Briton named William Samuel Henson secured a patent in 1843 for a proposed "aerial steam carriage," which Henson said would be ideal for "conveying letters, goods, and passengers from place to place" and which he later boasted would make it from London to "China in 24 hours certain."

Henson drew up elaborate and highly optimistic brochures with drawings of his great steam machine flying over exotic destinations such as the Great Pyramids of Egypt and the Taj Mahal. He even built a small model, featuring a cambered wing, a rudder, and two six-bladed propellers, but he could never persuade the venture capital firms of the day to part with the cash needed to build the real thing. And truthfully, it would have been all but impossible for Henson to succeed even if money had been no object: the sheer weight of the power source theoretically needed to generate steam to fly would have kept the contraption on the ground.

Still, Henson certainly deserves historical points for trying, as does another Briton and contemporary of his, George Hayward Cayley, a pioneering aeronauticist who applied far more scientific principles to the challenge of flight. Cayley, who lived from 1773 to 1857, was a keen observer of birds and bats, a physicist, and a highly skilled mathematician whose discoveries drew man ever closer to the grail of powered flight. He even designed his own "whirling arm," a rudimentary wind tunnel with which he could experiment how different kinds of wings would respond to the forces of air at various velocities and angles. "The whole problem is confined within these limits," he wrote, "to make a surface support a given weight by the application of power to the resistance of air."

In sum, it was dawning on the experts that the essential goal of powered flight would not ever be achieved, as had long been so vividly envisioned, by getting a pair of wings to flap up and down rapidly like those of a bird. In fact, concluded Sir Hiram Maxim, the American-born proprietor of the Maxim machine gun, it was "neither necessary nor practical to imitate the bird. Give us a motor and we will very soon give you a successful flying machine."

Maxim was right, and in retrospect it is astonishing to realize just how quickly the motor—the internal-combustion engine— expanded its utility from powering automobiles to enabling the Wright brothers to fly. The third of a century or so just after the U.S. Civil War was an incredible period for technological innovation, with American inventors often leading the way: the typewriter, the telephone, the phonograph, electric lights, the radio, and the camera all emerged in this time.

In travel, of course, the gasoline-powered engine quickly led to a novel concept, that people could actually move around without benefit of horse, boat, or train. But just as people were getting their minds around the idea of a mass-produced "automobile" (or *"Motorwagen,"* as German inventor Karl Benz called his vehicle) at the turn of the century, dreamers and inventors were wasting no time in a literal race to the sky.

It is much fun for us, knowing the outcome here on our side of history, to look back on just how widespread the skepticism was that man would indeed figure out how to fly. Shortly after the brilliant U.S. inventor Samuel Pierpont Langley crashed his "Aerodrome" (very loosely translated from the Greek as "air runner") in 1903, an eminent astronomer and physicist named Simon Newcomb put his finger on the apparent problem. Langley's models looked good, and he had received a combined $70,000 in grants from the War Department and the Smithsonian, a fortune at the time, to build a full-size aircraft with room for a sole pilot. Yet, Newcomb noted, the great Langley failed. Why?

"May not our mechanicians . . . be ultimately forced to admit that aerial flight is one of the great class of problems with which man can never cope, and give up all attempts to grapple with it?" Newcomb, the founding member and first president of the American Astronomical Society, asked in the October 22, 1903, issue of *The Independent.*

Even if a pilot could somehow get off the ground, Newcomb reasoned, it was nigh impossible to figure out how he could defy the forces of gravity for any sustained period of time.

"It is the speed alone that sustains him," Newcomb argued of his hypothetical flyer. "How is he ever going to stop? Once he slackens his speed, down he begins to fall. He may, indeed, increase the inclination of his aeroplane. Then he increases the resistance to the sustaining force. Once he stops he falls a dead mass. How shall he reach the ground without destroying his delicate machinery? I do not think the most imaginative inventor has yet even put upon paper a demonstratively successful way of meeting this difficulty."

The "only ray of hope," Newcomb said, now more than a bit sarcastically, was back with the birds again. "Quite likely the most effective flying-machine would be one carried by a vast number of little birds," he wrote. "Yes, a sufficient number of humming-birds, if we could combine their forces, would carry an aerial excursion party of human beings through the air."

Not two months after Newcomb's airy dismissal of the whole idea, the Wright brothers flew—and landed quite safely—at Kitty Hawk. To be fair to him, this pioneering astronomer did not conclude that manned flight would be impossible always and forever, but Newcomb did posit that the human race was a long ways off from figuring out all the angles. And in so arguing, he was just one among legions of experts who scoffed at the idea that success in flight was just waiting in the wings.

Nonetheless, on the Outer Banks of North Carolina on December 17, 1903, Orville and Wilbur Wright did it. The specific feat of these two bicycle builders from Ohio was to achieve manned, powered, controlled, heavier-than-air flight. The initial flight lasted just twelve seconds and 120 feet (by the end of the day their best was 852 feet, in fifty-nine seconds), and the Wright brothers did not achieve immediate acclaim. In fact, the first full account of their aerial accomplishments came not in the mass-circulation daily newspapers or in a popular science magazine, but in an account by a remarkably enterprising businessman and reporter named Amos Ives Root, writing in a beekeepers' journal called *Gleanings in Bee Culture.*

"These brothers have probably not even a faint glimpse of what their discovery is going to bring to the children of men," Root wrote in the January 1905 issue of *Gleanings.* "No one living can give a guess of what is coming along this line, much better than any one living could conjecture the final outcome of Columbus's experiment when he pushed off through the trackless waters. Possibly we may be able to fly over the North Pole . . ."

The Wright Flyer was in many ways the basic invention on top of which everything else was built, including the jet airplane. The brothers' flying machine was built from Sitka spruce wood and equipped with a four-cylinder engine that was both light enough and sufficiently powerful to drive a bicycle-style chain that in turn spun the twin propellers. The pilot—the brothers took turns—lay on his stomach, head facing forward, a gliderlike position that reduced drag on the machine and helped him to get and stay aloft. Once he was airborne a system of pulleys, in a cradle attached to the hip, allowed him not only to steer with the rudder but also to warp the wings, and thus exercise some command over the plane's natural inclination to roll (today's pilots use ailerons). Thus he could rise up and down, move left and right, and zoom forward over the windswept dunes. For the first time, in however rudimentary and precarious and brief a fashion, man could direct the course of his flight. It had taken the human race thousands of years to get to this step; in less than half a century, people would be able to step aboard a jet airliner and move at the unthinkable speed of 500 miles per hour. In England, the man who would build this airplane was already thinking about mechanical travel—the idea of closing the gap, of shortening the time needed to get between any two places on the maps that he kept all about him.

The story of this man, and of how Great Britain came to be the first nation to build a jetliner, begins with a little boy taking his toy parachute to the top window of a stone house and throwing it out, watching it float and twirl gently to the ground. It was a tiny piece of cloth, really, and it had come to him stuffed inside a Christmas cracker, the small, festively wrapped tube that opens with a loud snap and is a staple of British holidays. One day, however, "a miracle happened," or at least something that seemed a miracle to the young mind of Geoffrey de Havilland, staring out the window of a parsonage sometime in the middle of the 1880s on the outskirts of Nuneaton, a small industrial town in the county of Warwickshire, in the English Midlands. "Instead of falling directly to earth," de Havilland recalled many decades later, his toy parachute "started to rise, and went on rising until it passed over the stables in the yard. This was, of course, due to a local up-current of air, but even then seemed to have some special significance."

The boy, perhaps four or five at the time, might be indulged his fascination with a thing flying away, for the realities of his household were not altogether pleasant. His father was eccentric, as the polite phrasing goes, a minister who spent much of his day not tending to his flock, but cooped up in a moldy study, researching details of what he said would be a bombshell revelation that would bring many geographical errors of the Bible to light and "cause the history of the East to be rewritten," as he described it to his family. Nothing ever came of the great research project of the Reverend Charles de Havilland, and as the years passed he was increasingly given over to an obsession with hoarding. He plucked fine William pears from trees trained along the flint walls of the garden, but these were forbidden fruit. He laid them on the shelves of his study where they were ripened, but never eaten. If any of his five children would ask for a juicy pear, they always got the same answer from their father: "They require a few more days." The father never ate them, either, and he similarly hoarded the eggs from the Muscovy ducks wandering around the garden, laying them out on the shelves, to crack and mold and stink up the entire house.

"It was in this study, so often surrounded by rotten pears and eggs, that my father worked away at the book that was going to change history, or at least to reshape it," the boy with the parachute recalled. It is perhaps no surprise, then, that the boy would have a lifelong compulsion to travel elsewhere, to move, to fly, to get away. By the time he became an aviator, he had acquired an odd duality about him: an intense, evangelical, at times even charismatic passion for flight, walled off with periods of prolonged, detached silence. "In Geoffrey de Havilland," one friend explained, "you have that very rare mingling of ice and fire which enables the enthusiast to do long spells of quiet and constructive thinking."

He was born on July 27, 1882, at High Wycombe in Buckinghamshire, the second son of the Reverend Charles and Alice Jeannette de Havilland. The family lineage could be traced back to the days of William the Conqueror. When William invaded England in 1066, among the commanders of his army was the Sieur de Havylland (also spelled de Haverlain and de Haveilland), a knight who came from Lower Normandy and had a castle on the river Saire.

One branch of the powerful Lord of Haverland's family, spelling their name Haviland, eventually wound up in New York and Rhode Island, in the American colonies. Another, the de Havillands, became prominent in the south and east of England, not all that far from where William first attacked England. In a curious bit of a historical full circle, Geoffrey de Havilland's grandfather Charles wound up fighting in France, where he was taken prisoner by Napoleon.

Though his father was a clergyman and he had uncles who taught Latin and literature, Geoffrey de Havilland was fascinated from an early age by machinery, an interest that was encouraged heartily by his grandfather on his mother's side, Jason Saunders, a prosperous farmer and warehouse merchant who lived near Oxford.

When Geoffrey was a teenager, just before the turn of the

century, he was sent to a rectory near Gloucester, where his parents hoped the parson might at last steer him toward the proper profession.

"It was assumed at home that I should follow my father by entering the Church," de Havilland recalled in his autobiography, *Sky Fever*. But, he added, "when I considered the matter seriously I realized that all my interests centred [*sic*] on mechanical engineering, especially those dealing with motor-car design, something relatively new and exciting." Automobiles were still a rare sight, but one day Geoffrey and a friend of his pooled nearly all their savings and hired a car and driver for a ride to Newbury, about sixty miles away. Occasionally they all had to get out and push the vehicle uphill when the leather transmission belts slipped on their pulleys, and they were stuck at about 15 miles per hour on level stretches. Still, he remembered, they felt like explorers and attracted and intrigued applauding sightseers along the way.

"We had scarcely, in the popular phrase, annihilated space," Geoffrey said of the trip, his first in a car. "But after that short drive I knew that my future life lay in the world of mechanical travel." He thought the idea of travel, of shortening the time needed to get from place to place, was a natural human impulse—for him, this idea "gained a hold which was never to relax through all my working life."

The tensions between an ecclesiastically minded, unconventional father and a business-oriented, practical grandfather were among many sources of childhood unhappiness in the de Havilland household, for both Geoffrey and his older brother, Ivon, who was equally fascinated by things mechanical. There was, in fact, as Geoffrey put it, a sort of "withering scorn" the two main branches of his family felt for one another.

But this did not cloud either young man's mind in a choice of career. With the help and vigorous support of his grandfather, Geoffrey attended the Crystal Palace School of Engineering from 1900 to 1903, and held various jobs for a few years after that, designing both automobiles and motorcycles. Ivon, meanwhile, worked his way up through engineering jobs and by 1905 had designed a 12-horsepower, open-air touring car, the Iris, manufactured by Legros & Knowles of Willesden. The two brothers were very close and had planned to go into the automotive business together, designing and manufacturing cars, when the first of many tragedies struck in Geoffrey de Havilland's long life: Ivon died of influenza. He was twenty-six.

In his grief, and in a series of less than satisfactory design jobs after the death, Geoffrey's interest in automobiles actually began to wane. For years he was plagued by dreams in which his older brother reappeared to him, so powerfully real and yet acting so "secretive and strange before returning to an unknown place, lost to me again." Cars, still either a wondrous novelty or even an unknown invention to the vast majority of humanity, had somehow become a painful reminder of the past to Geoffrey de Havilland. He developed a new interest.

In 1908, Wilbur Wright brought a flying machine to Le Mans, in France. His demonstration was a sensation in Europe and, for de Havilland, himself now twenty-six, reading of this in his newspapers was the turning point. "Though I might never have seen an aircraft in the air," he said, "this was the machine to which I was prepared to give my life."

As it happened, de Havilland almost did give his life, the very next year, in de Havilland Biplane No. 1. This was a 45-horsepower, three-bay biplane that he designed and then built with a £1,000 loan from his enthusiastic grandfather and the help of an energetic and humorous good friend of his, Frank Hearle. Soon they had some critical assistance in building their aircraft. Frank had married de Havilland's younger sister, Ione, and Geoffrey had done some courting of his own. In visits back home to his parents' house, he had become enchanted with Louise Thomas, the governess to his younger siblings, a lively young woman whose eyes brightened when he talked of his inventions, even as she teased him about an enterprise as dangerous as flight. "Geoffrey," she would say, "I wish you could take up something more down-to-earth."

The men kept building. Ione kept the books and ran the house. Louie, as everyone called Geoffrey's new bride, hand-sewed every stitch of the stiff linen along the wings.

One perfect winter's day in 1909, near an old Roman encampment at Seven Barrows in Hampshire, de Havilland was ready to fly. From the top of a slight incline he ramped up the power of the twin propellers just behind him, then roared down the rough grass. Wider, wider, he opened the throttle and at last the moment had come. He pulled back hard on the stick and soon found himself and his plane go into the climb; but just after this moment when he had a wonderful sensation of lifting, and of looking upward at clear blue sky, he had another moment, the flash of knowledge that his thrilling angle of ascent meant he had made a terrible piloting mistake. In his elation, he had simply pulled back too hard and too fast.

"There was no time to correct the error," de Havilland said later of his first flight. "Before I could thrust the stick forward again, I heard the sound of snapping woodwork around me." The plane dropped quickly, hitting the ground with such force that it became a mass of shards, splinters, and torn fabric. De Havilland made another mistake by following his instinct to reassure those watching that he was all right. As he stood to motion to Hearle and to his younger brother, Hereward, that he was still alive, de Havilland was hit by a piece of airplane detritus that nearly sliced him at the wrist. Through the fog of a concussion, he saw the two men running toward him, and behind them the figure of his father. The Reverend de Havilland, as Geoffrey described it, "had hidden behind the shed pleading that he could not stand the strain of watching my first flight. He had, quite clearly, been right, and as soon as he was assured that I was alive he hastened home, speechless with shock."

While de Havilland's initial flying experience was not a triumph, human-powered flight was proceeding apace. By October 1905, the Wright brothers had managed to fly 24.5 miles in just under an hour, and by a few years after that, they had a patent—and a contract to make planes for the U.S. Army.

Records fell swiftly. It was an era later dubbed the Belle Époque of aviation. When Louis Blériot, a Frenchman, flew across the English Channel from Calais to Dover in July 1909, the first international flight ever, press baron Lord Northcliffe put this headline in his newspapers: "England No Longer an Island!" (Curiously, the Wright brothers passed on a clear opportunity for glory: Orville said that "exceptional feats"—he might as well have said "stunts"—were not consistent with the sober image of inventors that he and Wilbur wished to present in attracting investment for their company.) Later that year, in Reims, France, the first international air meet was held, with big crowds fascinated by the aerial races, sharp turns, and crazy loops executed by pilots in the exhibition.

In 1911, an American, thirty-two-year-old Cal Rodgers, became the first person to fly coast to coast across the United States. It took him eighty-four days, with nineteen crashes along the way, several of which put him in the local hospital. Rodgers's Wright brothers–built plane, the *Vin Fiz*, named for a grape drink marketed by the Chicago company that sponsored the trip, had a spruce airframe with canvas and linen coverings, a 35-horsepower engine, and no instruments other than a long shoelace, which Rodgers used to gauge vertical and horizontal motion. He navigated by following a special train with a white boxcar that contained numerous spare parts. The cockpit was exposed, and Rodgers smoked a cigar constantly, even as he flew.

Rodgers became a celebrity, though he missed out on a $50,000 prize (a little over $1 million in today's money) offered by publisher William Randolph Hearst to the first transcontinental flyer, since Hearst had stipulated it had to be done in thirty days or less. Just a few months after reaching the Pacific Ocean, the hero pilot was conducting a test flight in Long Beach,

California, in preparation for a cross-country return, when his airplane ran into a force that was to bedevil pilots up to the present day: a flock of birds. Smashing into the engine and the propeller, a crowd of gulls brought the airplane down for a crash landing in the Pacific. Rodgers died of a broken neck.

In 1916, a highly unofficial milestone was reached, the first reported incident in which people combined two especially sensory activities—flight and sex—into one supremely passionate act. Lawrence Sperry, a gifted pilot and mechanical genius, was giving a flying lesson to a wealthy socialite identified by the authorities as Mrs. Waldo Polk (Mr. Polk was in France at the time) on November 22, 1916, over Babylon, Long Island. The twenty-three-year-old Sperry was also experimenting with an invention of his called a gyroscopic stabilizer—essentially an autopilot—when all of a sudden, Sperry's Curtiss Flying Boat went into a steep dive and crashed into Great South Bay. Rescued by two duck hunters nearby, Sperry and Polk were found both dazed and naked, but police quickly discounted Sperry's assertion that their clothes had been completely ripped away by the force of the crash. Cynthia Polk, according to *The New York Times*, "asked that no word of the accident be conveyed to her relatives in New York, as it was trivial and she would soon be out of the hospital."

The *Times* was relatively discreet—"Mrs. W. Polk Hurt in Airship's Fall," said the headline—though the report, summarizing Sperry's and Polk's attempts to downplay the incident, did note rather archly that "both made light of the affair." But other newspapers had a field day with the naked-bodies angle, and

Sperry, according to his biographer, William Wyatt Davenport, later admitted to a friend and to his nephew that sex was indeed the precipitating cause of the accident. There was nothing wrong with either the plane or the autopilot. He, or she, had managed to bump into it at the height of ardor, shutting it off, and Sperry was "too entangled" to avert the problem before a crash landing. Today Sperry and Polk are generally recognized as the founding members of the "Mile High Club," for people who have had sex in flight, although technically their plane never flew above the 500-foot altitude at which Sperry had set his gyroscopic stabilizer.

For most people, of course, flight remained a curiosity, a daredevil sport, not a serious or practical form of transportation. As we will see in a later chapter, domestic air travel began in the United States as a means of carrying the mail, with passenger service taking many years to catch on as a profitable enterprise. Even then, it was an extremely uncomfortable one.

De Havilland was a man possessed, and he was a genius at designing airplanes. After his crash, he and Hearle fished the engine out of the wreck—nothing else was salvageable—and went to work on rebuilding the airplane. Just a few months later, they were back at Seven Barrows, and this time, with success. De Havilland grew so confident in his design that soon he had two frequent guests on board: Louie, and Geoffrey Raoul, their new son, the firstborn child, who, as the proud father put it, "arriv[ed] in this world as I was beginning to fly farther and higher than ever before."

There was, of course, no one around to teach the engineer how to fly. That was something he figured out as he built the airplanes. He quickly gained renown for his skill, and in 1911 he was hired by the British War Office, which appointed him a pilot and aircraft designer at His Majesty's Balloon Factory, the predecessor agency to the Royal Aircraft Establishment. By 1914, the government had an urgent need for his expertise. Great Britain was at war.

The BE-2, de Havilland's first warplane, was a modification of a "Blériot Experimental" plane built by the great French flyer, and hence its initials. Soon, however, Geoffrey de Havilland came up with a complete redesign, with greater stability and a flexible design that allowed this new plane, the BE-2c, to be used as a fighter, a bomber, an interceptor, or a reconnaissance craft.

All told, some thirty-five hundred variants of this de Havilland plane were built in World War I, by twenty different manufacturers, some as far away as Australia. About one-third of the total Allied air strength lay in his planes and in the United States, 95 percent of wartime airplanes constructed were of the de Havilland design.

De Havilland's unique mind was needed for yet another reason. For the British population, World War I had brought a new and especially terrifying menace to the home front: the Zeppelins. These huge German airships, for which the Allies had no early equivalent, represented the first time in history that a military power had the ability to carry out indiscriminate bombing from the sky across a civilian population. Many German commanders meant to take full advantage, and they believed Count Zeppelin's invention was a crucial psychological weapon as well. In 1914, Konteradmiral Paul Behncke explained to his superiors that bombardments across the London area would inflict not just physical damage, but would "cause panic in the population which may possibly render it doubtful that the war can be continued."

In that same year, German schoolchildren were taught to sing a song that included the lines: "Fly, Zeppelin! Help us win the war, England shall be destroyed with fire. Zeppelin, fly!"

The idea of civilian bombardment was ghastly, and at first the Kaiser, who through royal intermarriage had plenty of British relatives, resisted it. He ordered that only military installations on British soil should be bombed from the sky. But his generals were insistent: Really, why was aerial bombardment of civilians any morally worse than the noose the Allies were trying to draw around Germany, a land and naval blockade that could starve civilians?

In 1915, the Zeppelins began dropping bombs, both on London and on farms and town squares in the English countryside. For the British, whose island nation had not been successfully attacked since the 1066 assault by William the Conqueror, the fire raining from the sky was a severe shock. The Royal Navy, which had for so long kept England untouchable, was utterly useless against this new mass weapon. German newspapers were jubilant. One editorialized: "It has come to pass—that which the English have long feared and have repeatedly contemplated with terror. The most modern air weapon, a triumph of German inventiveness and the sole possession of the German military, has shown itself capable of crossing the sea and carrying the war right to the sod of old England!"

In one important way, the Zeppelin bombings had the reverse effect of what the German military masters intended. When a British captain named Oscar Grieg was taken captive after an aerial dogfight near Douai, in France, he struck a decidedly defiant note when his German interrogator asked him what he thought of the mighty Zeppelin force.

"Splendid!" Grieg said, according to the German's notes. "Best thing they have ever done, as recruits were now coming in so fast that we hardly knew how to deal with them."

Still, the Zeppelin raids would claim two thousand civilian casualties, cause hundreds of millions of pounds' worth of damage, and strike precisely the sort of fear and panic the Germans intended. Conventional land-based weapons could not reach these ships of death up in the sky; for that, the British turned to Geoffrey de Havilland.

The boost to national morale was simply tremendous when, after more than a year and a half of unchecked Zeppelin attacks, a converted de Havilland plane shot down one of the giant German airships. This occurred at about two-fifteen a.m. on September 3, 1916, when Lieutenant William Leefe Robinson, heading toward the glow of a huge fire in northeast London caused by a bomb from one of sixteen German airships involved in a mass raid, picked up a dim image ahead of him. It was the wooden-framed Schütte-Lanz SL11, partially illuminated by searchlights, floating over Cuffley, Hertfordshire, and readying to go home toward Germany. Robinson, with no oxygen aboard, straining his BE-2c to its maximum altitude of near 13,000 feet, closed to 500 feet from the airship and let go with a blast of machine-gun bullets.

The airship abruptly burst into flames and crashed behind the Plough Inn at Cuffley, killing all sixteen men aboard. The flash of the explosion was visible for miles, and though it was the middle of the night, thousands who had been terrorized by the raid watched as the huge enemy craft was blown to bits.

Henry Tuttle, ten years old at the time, was an eyewitness to the hit and later recalled it this way: "It was a fantastic sight like a big silver cigar and it seemed to be going very slowly by this time. A lot of people came out of their houses and then all of a sudden flames started to come from the Zeppelin and then it broke in half and was one mass of flames. It was an incredible sight: people were cheering, dancing, singing and somebody started playing the bagpipes. This went on, well into the night."

Not every British citizen was so jubilant. A woman named Sybil Morrison watched the same crash as Tuttle and felt sickened, both by the event and the reaction. "It was like a big cigar, I suppose," she said with "roaring flames—blue, red, purple." The young German men on board "were being roasted to death. Of course you weren't supposed to feel any pity for your enemies, nevertheless I was appalled to see the kind, good-hearted British people dancing about in the streets at the sight . . . clapping and singing and cheering. And my own friends: Delighted! When I said I was appalled that anyone could be pleased to see such a terrible sight, they said: 'But they're Germans. They're the enemy, not human beings.' And it was like a flash to me that that was what war did; it created this inhumanity in perfectly decent, nice, gentle, kindly people."

Over the next few months, pilots on de Havilland planes shot down five more German airships, and despite the revulsion felt by people like Morrison, the overall effect was to provide an incalculable shot of national morale.

The pressure on de Havilland was enormous; as astonishing as his gains were in an industry that had scarcely existed a few years before, his German competitors were no less inventive and in some ways, by the middle of the war, were clearly superior. RAF pilots began to complain that the BE-2s could not hold their own against the Fokker Eindecker combat planes the Germans unleashed in 1916. "Fokker fodder" was a derisive nickname some British papers began to give de Havilland's planes; Imperial German air pilots called them *kaltes Fleisch*, or cold meat. One British pilot called the BE-2 "a bloody awful aeroplane," and Parliament ordered a judicial inquiry into the airpower deficit. Geoffrey de Havilland had been pushed by his country's leaders to deliver as well and as quickly as possible, a pattern that would be replicated a generation later with the jet Comet. As World War I came to a close, de Havilland was not only unappreciated; now he was being vilified.

Though the inquiry ultimately absolved him of any blame and the Allies won the war, the stress and exhaustion were so severe that by mid-1918, just months before the Armistice, Geoffrey de Havilland suffered a nervous breakdown. He had endured profound melancholy before, especially when his brother died; he had certainly worked himself to the far physical edge. This was a complete collapse, in both mind and body. Doctors ordered him to months of strict rest in a nursing home.

"I recalled the periods of depression of earlier days," de Havilland wrote later, "but at least they had been only brief, whereas this was now almost continuous."

To the doctors, it was unclear whether he could ever function normally again. In retrospect, though, this was one of those long periods of icy silence that his friend would describe so well. At first, alone, in a room in the quiet pallor of a rest home, Geoffrey de Havilland played it all over in his mind, over and over again. It was like an endlessly skipping phonograph, something today's psychiatrists diagnose as a "ruminative loop" of anxiety and self-recrimination. How had his marvelous invention gone so wrong?

Ever so slowly, though, the loop dissolved. Color, perspective, and even humor returned to him. He became well enough to leave; Louie found a house for them and their three boys, in Stanmore, near his oldest and best friends. The compulsion, it turned out, had never left him—de Havilland was determined to fly again, in planes he would build, better and faster and safer than ever. It was 1920. The war was over. It was time to begin again. He had an announcement. The de Havilland Aircraft Company was open for business.

"I was able to do some of my best and most strenuous work in design and flying in the years that followed," he wrote later in his autobiography, *Sky Fever*—whose title seems all the more apt in light of his period of mental difficulties. "But the illness has been a severe warning," he added, "that there were definite limits beyond which I must never again trespass."

Over the course of a long career, de Havilland never lacked for vivid names to give his aircraft. There was an entire array of Moths: the Gipsy Moth, the Cirrus Moth, Hawk Moth, the Tiger Moth, the Fox Moth, the Leopard Moth. He built fighters called the Vampire, the Vixen, and the Venom. In 1934, he designed a twin-engine plane for the MacRobertson Trophy Air Race, the longest course in the world. The route stretched from Mildenhall in England to Melbourne, Australia, with five compulsory clock-in stops—Baghdad, Allahabad, Singapore, and the two Australian cities of Darwin and Charleville—and twenty-two optional but much-needed ones laid in with fuel, oil, and food. The World's Greatest Air Race helped to celebrate the centenary of Melbourne and it highlighted the increasing air-mindedness of Australia. It carried a prize of $75,000 put up by Sir Macpherson Robertson, and it was excellent advertising for the confectionary company he owned.

Of the twenty aircraft that made the final cut, three were de Havilland's, and he called this racer the Comet—a name that so struck his fancy that he would use it again, for his jet airliner. There was an American-built DC-2, flying in the livery of the Dutch airline KLM, and a Boeing 247, sponsored by an American film studio, Warner Bros.

It was a brutal and literally deadly race. A small British plane crashed near Palazzo San Gervasio in Italy, killing both members of the crew. Another British plane, the Airspeed AS.8 Viceroy, withdrew with brake trouble at Athens. An Australian Lockheed Vega plane named the "Puck" overturned on landing at Aleppo, in Syria, sparing the crew any major injuries but bowing out of the race. The KLM plane, named the Uiver, got lost in a series of Australian thunder showers, only to be rescued by a postal clerk in Albury, New South Wales, who flipped the town lights on and off to signal "Albury" by Morse code. A radio announcer appealed for cars to drive to the airstrip and light up the way, and the Uiver landed safely. When the rain let up, the local townspeople helped to drag the DC-2 out of the muck and onto the runway. It was back in the race. (KLM later made a donation of gratitude to the Albury hospital, and the town mayor was awarded a Dutch noble title.)

The Boeing 247 came in third, with an elapsed flying time of ninety-two hours, fifty-five minutes, and the KLM DC-2, despite its wayward course over Australia, took second in ninety hours, thirteen minutes. But the runaway winner, in seventy-one hours flat, was a de Havilland Comet, the scarlet "Grosvenor House," flown by a British crew and named for a London hotel. For Geoffrey de Havilland, it was an international triumph. It marked the first time, but not the last, that one of his airplanes would engage in direct competition with the American aircraft manufacturing powers. In 1938, de Havilland introduced the twin-engine, seventeen-passenger DH 95 Flamingo, its first all-metal airplane and one considered capable of going into a pitched sales battle with the Douglas DC-3. Now the United States and Great Britain would vie for the attention of the world's leading airlines. But this friendly battle was never joined, because World War II quickly put the issue of civilian airliner sales on hold.

The exigencies of geography meant that the United Kingdom and the United States would develop somewhat different priorities in the war years, and emerge from them with different areas of expertise. After the Japanese attack on Pearl Harbor, the Americans did not have to worry too much about an invasion on the continental home front, and they put much focus on large, long-range transports and bombers that could take the fight to far-flung battlefields. They came out of the war with some magnificent four-engine propeller-driven airplanes, and no huge sense of urgency among the commercial air carriers about jumping into the Jet Age.

For the United Kingdom, as Churchill's wartime cable about the German jet fighter amply demonstrated, the strange new power of the jet engine represented a much more direct threat.

The tide of war had turned strongly in the Allies' favor by 1944, but the Nazis' screaming jet plane was a giant and mysterious wild card. Like the German Zeppelins of World War I, the Messerschmitts of this war could pose a new, unchecked menace to the British population. The Allies were fortunate in one respect: as Hitler argued with his Luftwaffe commanders over the specifications of the jet, pushing them to make it bigger and give it massive capacity for bombs, the Germans had delayed putting it into battle by several months. But now the Nazis were flying the first operational jet in history, and though the British were racing to perfect their own jet fighters, the prime minister knew the Germans were ahead with the basic technology. Thus his blunt, six-word command: "Catch up as soon as possible." Yet again, the urgency of war was driving man to risky new heights.

The jet engine took more than twenty years of work, thought, design, trials, and errors before anyone used it successfully to propel an airplane. For much of that time the very concept, as with human-powered flight itself, endured a fantastic amount of skepticism from academic experts, government leaders, and the private marketplace. It was such a complicated piece of machinery that history has settled on not one, but two, inventors of the technology—two men working in two nations and on two different sides of World War II. At first, neither had any deep knowledge of the other's work, and it was not until well after the war that Frank Whittle of England and Hans von Ohain of Germany met to discuss their mutual, signal innovation. Late in life, both living in the United States, they became good friends.

Even without direct contact, each man's mind worked along similar lines, with Whittle being first to design the jet engine but von Ohain coming in first in the race, literally, to make it fly with an airplane attached to it. "The tree of scientific knowledge tends to bear its fruit at the same time," Whittle said many years later. As Whittle explained it, a jet engine could work "something like a giant vacuum cleaner; it sucks air at the front and blows it out at the back." But for this brilliant young RAF flyer and engineer, the general reaction to his early conception of the jet was crystallized by one of his professors of aeronautical engineering, at Cambridge University, to whom he had shown drawings for a theoretical engine that would fire a series of jet nozzles to provide blasts of supercharged air power to an airplane.

"Very interesting, Whittle my boy," the professor said. "But it will never work!"

The jet engine was to its propeller predecessor what a fire hose is to a garden hose. Standard propellers had two or three curved blades, and thus a natural limit to their power and speed, even when designers started mounting multiple engines on the wings. In the 1930s, Whittle and von Ohain both started applying principles of physics to a different and potentially far more potent way to provide thrust to airplanes. Rather than firing an engine to turn the external blades of a propeller, they reasoned, an engine might be designed to spin the internal blades of a turbine. If air could be compressed inside the engine and fired with fuel and pushed out of a nozzle, the rearward force would be tremendous—a stream of supercharged air more concentrated and more powerful than the airstream generated by propeller.

Whittle filed for a patent in 1930 and got it two years later, and here and there received some money from London venture capitalists. "The impression he made was overwhelming," one of them enthused in 1935 about the twenty-eight-year-old engineer. "This was genius, not [just] talent. Whittle expressed his idea with superb conciseness: 'Reciprocating engines are exhausted. They have hundreds of parts jerking to and fro, and they cannot be made more powerful without becoming too complicated. The engine of the future must produce 2,000 horsepower with one moving part: a spinning turbine and compressor.'"

Far easier said than done, of course, and Whittle's money ran down. No one in the government would stick his neck out for the unproven jet technology: in fact, because he was still an officer with the RAF, which was paying for him to study at Cambridge, he actually needed official dispensation to work on his outside design project. No more than six hours a week, his RAF superiors told him.

"For the most part I met with blank astonishment," said Whittle, "and told I was asking for a combustion intensity at least twenty times greater than had ever been achieved." Whittle finished up his studies and eventually got permission to devote full-time attention to his company, Power Jets Ltd. He drove himself relentlessly, twice setting the barn where he did his research on fire and finally, in April 1937, getting his "Whittle Unit" engine to fire a steady stream of jet power for twenty minutes, uninterrupted, in the laboratory. At one point he and his colleagues became alarmed when this bench unit kept accelerating—even after they had shut down the fuel pump. What had they wrought? Closer investigation determined that the engine had a fuel leak, so that it was running even on the fuel spilled inside the unit; when that burned off, finally, the engine shut down. Impressive, but highly dangerous in an actual flight situation. His financial supporters said it was too expensive without government involvement, but the Air Ministry debated nearly a year before releasing the relatively small amount of £5,000 for work on a flyable design. In retrospect, the British squandered a lead, and it was only after war with Germany broke out that the government decided on the urgency of the matter.

Finally, Whittle, a short, wiry, intense man with a droopy mustache and an occasionally fierce temper, had the support he needed to pursue his ideas fully. With the UK at war, he drove his staff relentlessly, but he was hardest on himself. He smoked three packs of cigarettes a day and he sniffed Benzedrine as a stimulant during workdays that could stretch to eighteen hours, then downed tranquilizers and sleeping medications to bring himself down for the night. His weight dropped to 127 pounds, and his temper was getting worse.

"The responsibility that rests on my shoulders is very heavy indeed," he confessed to his diary. "Either we place a powerful new weapon in the hands of the Royal Air Force or, if we fail to get our results in time, we may have falsely raised hopes." In that case, he worried, he might have deprived the war effort of hundreds of conventional airplanes that could have been built instead.

"I have a good crowd 'round me," he added—praise that he seemed more inclined to deliver on paper, to himself, than to the people themselves. "They are all working like slaves, so much so, that there is a risk of mistakes through physical and mental fatigue."

In Germany, Hans von Ohain found a much more steady and enthusiastic source of support: from industrialist Ernst Heinkel, who had built up a large aircraft company despite curbs on German airplane manufacturing imposed by the Treaty of Versailles after World War I. Heinkel initially developed his expertise with contracts abroad, including one to develop catapult-launch seaplanes for the Imperial Japanese Navy. In the 1930s, the Nazi-led Luftwaffe snapped up Heinkel planes and thus funneled money into the research arm of the company. Early on the morning of August 27, 1939, just days before Hitler invaded Poland, a small single-pilot airplane with a metal fuselage, overhead wooden wings, and a single jet engine buried into its nose roared down the runway at an aerodrome outside Rostock.

"The hideous wail of the engine was music to our ears," said Heinkel. The plane, piloted by Erich Warsitz, was in the air for just six minutes in the skies over Germany, but in that time the He 178 took its place as the first jet-powered airplane in history.

Whittle's engine, attached to a small Gloster E28/29 airframe, also managed to succeed, for seventeen minutes, reaching a top speed of 370 miles per hour—but this was not until 1941. "Frank, it flies!" a colleague at the RAF base in Cranwell said to him with a hearty pat on the back. "Well, that's what it was bloody well designed to do, wasn't it?" Whittle replied. Even at this point, having gotten jet-powered planes into the air, both the British and the Germans were racing to overcome enormous technological hurdles to make the planes operational—and useful in combat. The engines ran dreadfully hot, posing risks of fire or melting damage to the metal, and they consumed an insane amount of fuel, so much so that they could barely stay in the air for twenty minutes. Furthermore, the early engines could not reliably attain the speed that was intended to be their big advantage to begin with. They were of questionable use in war—or in peace, for that matter.

German researchers overcame several of these hurdles through improvements in compression and air-cooling tubes, and by putting two engines on a fighter fuselage they came up with a plane that could fly for about forty minutes but was still subject to catching fire and was frightfully difficult to bring in for a landing. By the autumn of 1943, the Messerschmitt Me 262 was ready for production; it would become the first operational jet of the war and of history, the screaming, shark-like intruder that the two RAF pilots would encounter the following summer over Munich.

But for the German builders, there was an added problem: just as they were succeeding in getting this jet fighter ready for the assembly line, word abruptly came from Hitler that they must make it bigger and heavier. The Führer wanted a jet bomber, with bays for two 550-pound bombs; even as the Allies pressed in on him and many of his generals argued that the main issue would be defense of the Reich, he was planning for an all-out offensive; another blitz on England.

"It is imperative that the Luftwaffe have a number of jet fighter-bombers ready for front commitment by the spring of 1944," Hitler ordered, late in 1943. Production was held up for several months while engineers worked to accommodate the new specifications.

That delay was, in retrospect, an important piece of good fortune for the Allies, for it involved several critical months in which the advantage in the war grew strongly in their favor, making the ultimate introduction of the German jet much less of a threat than it might have been. Coordinated attacks by British and U.S. air forces in February 1944 inflicted severe damage on the Messerschmitt plant in Augsburg where the bigger plane was being tested. German supply routes were being methodically cut off as well, so many of the Me 262s were built of severely deficient materials. The net result was that while the Germans produced slightly more than fourteen hundred Me 262s during the war, less than three hundred of those actually engaged in combat. Training in the single-seat jets was effectively a learn-as-you-go process, with predictably deadly results. One Luftwaffe official said after the war that the Me 262s thus wound up killing many more Germans than Allies.

For all those problems, however, the Me 262 was an impressive aeronautical achievement—and an important first in aviation history. In most respects, German jet technology and research was more advanced than that of the Allies during the war, though that only became clear after the war was over, and it was certainly not Frank Whittle's fault. He got far less help and support at the outset from the British government than von Ohain received in Germany.

Had Hitler and the Luftwaffe pressed this lead harder, could it have altered the outcome of the conflict? Perhaps, but the weight of the evidence suggests otherwise.

True, an earlier and more impressive jet fighter in the Nazi arsenal might have yielded a tremendous psychological advantage. Any jet whatsoever—even a brief appearance by that first, tiny, experimental Heinkel jet—would have been an astounding propaganda coup for the Nazis in 1940, when they were conducting the punishing air raids on the United Kingdom that marked the Battle of Britain. So, in theory, it might have given ammunition to Hitler's plan for an alleged "armistice" that would have halted his aerial bombing of the UK and left most of continental Europe under the Nazi boot.

But by itself, Germany's lead in jet technology was really never great enough to change the basic direction of the war, and even by the end, when each side had fighter jets to deploy, such airplanes amounted to well under 1 percent of the total numbers of aircraft.

Moreover, it's implausible that a leader such as Churchill would have allowed the appearance of a small Nazi jet, however terrifying, to be a decisive factor even when the chips were down, which they most certainly were for the British in 1940. He was rallying the British people to fight "the odious apparatus of Nazi rule," and this was the year of his greatest exhortations: "I have nothing to offer but blood, toil, tears and sweat," and "Let us therefore brace ourselves to our duties, and so bear ourselves that, if the British Empire and its Commonwealth last for a thousand years, men will still say, 'This was their finest hour.'"

If the Heinkel jet had flown over London, it would not have changed the prime minister's resolve. It would have become yet another challenge for the Allies to match, another blow in a terrible year that saw the evacuation of the British Expeditionary Force at Dunkirk and the surrender of France to the Nazis. It most likely would not have altered a word of the speech he gave to Parliament on June 4, 1940, less than a month after he took the leader's office: "We shall fight on the seas and oceans, we shall fight with growing confidence and growing strength in the air, we shall defend our Island, whatever the cost may be, we shall fight on the beaches, we shall fight on the landing grounds, we shall fight in the fields and in the streets, we shall fight in the hills; we shall never surrender."

As it happened, despite their technological lead, it would take the Germans another few years to get their jets into production mode. And, as impressive as that achievement was, it was certainly a clear case of too little, too late in terms of the Me 262 reversing the course of the conflict. By 1945, even with the Me 262 in the skies and menacing the slower planes of Allied pilots such as Lobban and Wall, the RAF men in a de Havilland Mosquito, the Allies were on a clear path to victory.

By the end of the war, both the British and the Americans had jet fighters, although none ever met the Me 262 in the air. The first jet-on-jet dogfight would not occur until the Korean War. And, with defeat, Germany was forbidden to manufacture aircraft—all of its knowledge in the field was essentially turned over, with the fruits of the research now available to the best of the British and American companies—and to an emergent Soviet power. What had been a wartime race between the Nazis and the Allies now was a peacetime struggle among Great Britain, the United States, and the Soviet Union.

"The scale on which science and engineering have been harnessed to the chariot of destruction is indeed amazing," Richard Clarkson, the chief aerodynamicist for the de Havilland company, said after a survey of German military air facilities just after V-E Day. "We in the civil aviation field will indeed be lucky in the postwar era in not meeting competition from the vanquished Germans." With the Germans out, the UK aviation industry now had an opportunity. With Geoffrey de Havilland leading the way, the British were determined to seize it.

four

Empires in the Sky

Bill Allen

As World War II drew to a close, the Boeing Airplane Company was in a paradoxical situation for a firm that had been such a huge part of the successful military effort. For Boeing, victory meant loss—loss of military contracts, loss of jobs. In Seattle, victory meant that Boeing would have to cut 15,000 jobs from the wartime peak of 46,000 and, based on the projections for postwar military spending, it was likely to have to cut another 15,000. This was, in itself, a challenge, but Boeing was also in a crisis. Its leader, Phil Johnson, was gone.

Philip Gustav Johnson, the son of Swedish immigrants, was a brilliant engineer who, like many of the company's best and most creative designers, was hired directly by Bill Boeing out of the University of Washington. He had risen from draftsman to president in less than a decade and had driven himself relentlessly, turning one part of the Boeing empire into United Air Lines, then picking up another and helping the United States to fight and win a war. Johnson led the Seattle-based Boeing Airplane Company through its massive production of military planes in World War II. But with the war nearly over and clearly won, all the Herculean toil caught up with the man behind the B-17 and the B-29 Superfortress and all the other big wartime bombers. He collapsed one day in his Wichita hotel room. Two months shy of his fiftieth birthday, Phil Johnson was dead of a cerebral hemorrhage.

There was no clear leader in sight to take his place. Bill Boeing himself was out. The big man with the trademark mustache was certainly still young enough, at sixty-four, to come back and run the business for a while, but he was far too fed up even to consider such a thing.

Boeing, the timber and mining baron whose 1914 flight over Lake Washington left him so enthusiastic that he decided to launch his own aircraft company, had certainly left his imprint on the company that bore his name. It was largely known as a military contractor, and this accorded with the founder's belief in military preparedness, which was so fervent that he had done a most unusual thing shortly before the United States got involved in World War I.

One day, Boeing flew over downtown Seattle and began dropping hundreds of red cardboard propaganda leaflets shaped like artillery shells. The fake shells rained down on the Seattle streets, and pedestrians who plucked them up found an impassioned warning printed on them: the United States, said the cardboard shells, was woefully short of airplanes and utterly unprepared to defend itself against an aerial attack. "For national defense, encourage aviation," they said. "Our country needs more airplanes!" A few weeks later, he did it again, this time over a packed stadium of fans watching a football game between the University of Washington and the University of California. "Protection Through Preparedness," this bomb proclaimed. "This harmless card in the hands of a hostile foe might have been a bomb dropped upon you. Aeroplanes"—here he used the alternative spelling of the word—"are your defense!!! Aero Club of the Northwest." (Curiously, Bill Boeing would turn out not to be Seattle's only Ivy League dropout-turned-mogul with a flair for the dramatic: in 2009, Bill Gates, the Microsoft cofounder and philanthropist, unleashed a jar of mosquitoes at a gathering of technology leaders to make a point that there was "no reason only poor people should be infected" with malaria. With both the crowd and the mosquitoes buzzing, Gates paused a few moments before reassuring everyone that the flying insects did not actually harbor the disease.)

With a kick-start from the military and a genius for snapping up air mail contracts, Bill Boeing had built up a giant company in Seattle. There were Boeing airplanes, Boeing engines, even a Boeing airline. But Boeing's company was too giant, decided Franklin D. Roosevelt and the New Deal trust-busters, and it was split in three in 1934, just like that. One branch became United Air Lines, another became United Aircraft Corporation, an East Coast engine manufacturer and precursor to United Technologies. The third unit, retaining both the name of the Boeing Airplane Company and its Seattle base, was the airplane builder.

But Bill Boeing quit in disgust, and he made—and largely kept—a vow to stay out of the airplane business. When he died aboard his yacht in 1956, three days shy of his seventy-fifth birthday, he was worth $22 million—but not a penny of it was in Boeing stock.

In any event, the company's board and the company's founder never had a serious discussion about his coming back, and now, in 1945, the Boeing board had been looking about for months for a new leader. Johnson's death in September of the year before had stunned people in both the airplane and airline businesses, and not just because of his youth. For as much as he was respected for his wartime leadership, Phil Johnson was the man who was going to figure out Boeing's postwar future. The company needed a strategy: even as the United States was celebrating surrender by both the Germans and the Japanese in 1945, the mood in Seattle was quickly turning bitter.

"I tell you, folks, the best thing you can do is go back to Iowa," one man shouted at a Seattle Chamber of Commerce meeting about the situation, shaking his finger at a Boeing official seated on a dais. "I know these people aren't going back to work at Boeing, and you know it." Another man called for a government takeover of Boeing. The official the crowd was shouting at was the company's new president, Bill Allen.

Allen was disciplined, and one of his rules was to never lose his temper, at least in public. Privately, he shared much of the despair. In a period of two months, $1.5 billion in contracts had been canceled, nearly 38,000 workers laid off, and one of Boeing's big plants in Wichita, Kansas, had to be shut down altogether. "My Lord," Allen confided to a friend, "the roof has fallen in."

The man the Boeing board turned to was an unlikely titan for the aviation industry. He was a partner in a Seattle law firm, with no training in either engineering or manufacturing, and no prior executive experience. Bill Allen was lacking in all these areas, and he was still in deep grief over the loss of his wife to cancer just two years before. Yet for all the credentials Bill Allen didn't have, there was something the Boeing board knew that weighed heavily in his favor.

Allen was clearly a man of good judgment and a natural, if often quiet, leader. Allen had started out drafting the legal papers for Bill Boeing's timber business and the aircraft company, but it was not long before Boeing and others sought out his opinion on all kinds of matters. In the months before Johnson's death, he had leaned, more and more, on Bill Allen for support and judgment, and the board knew it. More than anything, Allen had the ability to get people in a room and sort out complicated decisions; as one historian of the Boeing company later put it, "Allen knew how to lead by listening."

As he would do for much of his life, Allen confided to a diary and the lawyer in him made up yet another one of his endless lists, the arguments pro and con, the issues to be weighed by the judge and jury of his mind. There wasn't much to be said in the "pro" column: there was "a little greater material return" than an already highly lucrative law salary; there was the idea, of course, of a "new challenge" to take on. But he could think of plenty of reasons to say no to Boeing's offer. For one thing: "I do not feel I have the qualifications. That's the all-compelling reason."

As a widower, he recognized that his daughters, who were ten and five, needed him. "Heaven knows I have little enough time for them now," he wrote. "They need the time I give them and more, too." The salary was no big draw; his firm was making plenty of money. Not only were military contracts due to be slashed, but the unity of the war effort had postponed the inevitable dispute with Boeing's labor unions over a fair wage.

"Trouble lies ahead," Allen predicted privately, correctly. He took the job.

Allen took an almost mischievous delight in getting engineers, who spoke in complex mathematical and physical terms to each other, to explain their rationales in simpler terms, which in turn helped the sales force to go out and sell the Boeing product to customers. "I'm just a lawyer," he'd say, scribbling on his legal pad, asking for clarifications. "Explain that to me again. Make it shorter this time."

Recalled George Schairer, a brilliant aerodynamicist and one of the leading designers of the 707: "Bill was a very interesting guy. Anytime there was a big decision to be made, he would call all the interested parties in and he'd go around the table asking for opinions.

"He'd turn to the first person and just go all the way around the table without saying anything himself," Schairer said in an interview for a company oral history project many years later. "He'd just sit there writing. . . . As each spoke, Allen wouldn't say anything himself except to ask a question now and then. He refused to make any decision, or provide any leadership, until he had gone completely around the table listening to everyone have his say."

Allen was smart, ambitious, and charming, though deceptively self-mocking in public. He joked that he spent much of his college career "sitting around sorority houses" at the University of Montana in Missoula, but somehow Bill Allen of small-town Montana found his way to Harvard Law School, picking up his degree in 1925. Though he had plenty of offers from firms in the East, his heart remained out West and, in Missoula in 1927, he married Dorothy Dixon, the daughter of the governor of the state of Montana. And though he spent most of his career in Seattle, Allen retained a touching, if somewhat outsized, love of his native state: anybody from Montana, he always told his secretaries, could get in to see him, anytime, no appointment needed.

By far the biggest decision that Bill Allen had to make was whether the company should jump into the jet airliner business. With a new generation of Cold War jet bombers divided up among several American manufacturers, Boeing had decided to go after a military contract for a large, four-engine jet tanker that could provide aerial refueling and cargo services. And it had developed an important, if expensive, advantage as it headed toward a decision: a huge wind tunnel in Seattle that could be used for aerodynamic testing near the speed of sound. Schairer, one of many industry experts who were rushed into Germany at the end of the war to study the Luftwaffe's research, found a stunning affirmation of a concept that Boeing had also been exploring: the swept wing.

Up to that point, most airplanes had been designed with wings more or less perpendicular to the fuselage, which worked fine with propeller-driven engines. But as jet engines made the planes faster, approaching the speed of sound, the conventional wing began to act as more of a drag on forward motion. By angling the wings backward, designers could cut the drag and position the engines in a better path to perform their main function, which was to provide thrust. The wind tunnel was of profound importance in developing the swept-wing B-47 Stratojet, a six-engine bomber, and that research in turn laid the groundwork for design of the Dash-80.

But it was a calculation to be made literally by degrees, or fractions of degrees. Boeing tested sixty-eight different types of wings more than 27,000 hours, ultimately settling on a 35-degree sweep, and the engineering team added yet another innovation. Schairer and George Martin, the chief designer, had also used wind-tunnel testing to figure out the optimal location for engines: they did not need to be buried into the wing, as British Comet designers would decide, but could hang down on struts. This placement made the engines much easier to maintain or replace, and over time became the standard for jetliners except, of course, for those with engines along the tail.

But even with all these improvements, the simple fact of the matter was that jet engines consumed far more fuel than their propeller counterparts and no one could promise at that point to provide an airliner configuration that could make it across the ocean nonstop. That obviously undercut the main advantage of the jet—speed—and made U.S. airlines extremely leery of committing to buy a jetliner.

In the 1940s, Boeing engineers wound up crafting several different renderings on paper for a jet airliner, which in retrospect were fairly prescient suggestions of jetliners to come, but far too early to entice any airline to buy. One from December 1946, by W. L. Kellerman, had an overhead swept wing and a swept tail, with side-by-side jets in a pod on either side (four engines in all).

But as the 1940s gave way to the 1950s, no one in the United States seemed to be clamoring for a jet—no airline executives, no passengers. "In the popular mind, jets were still demonstrably machines of war," observed Clive Irving, a British journalist and aviation historian. "They had manners to match—they were thunderous in sound and left smutty trails behind them. It required a leap of imagination to think that they might be house-trained to the point where they could use civilian airports without befouling them and scaring the neighborhood out of its wits."

Bill Allen tried his best. He courted Trippe and Hughes, as well as the presidents of American and United. He got close with Pan Am, even drawing up a contract in September 1949 for six "new Boeing Jet Transport Aircraft," which would have been known to the world as the Boeing 473 and cost about $4 million apiece. But Trippe balked at inking the deal: it was simply too much money for an as-yet unproven concept. "Wait and see" seemed to be the industry motto.

The airlines, having invested hundreds of millions of dollars in the postwar period in the latest generation of propeller planes, were extremely hesitant. They were making good money flying those planes; why trade that for the uncertainties of the jetliner? An enormous number of objections to jets were raised, beyond those of safety and cost. They were too loud. They were too fast—so much so that air-traffic controllers might not be able to keep track of them on radar. "There is a limit on how many blips a single brain can safely juggle," a *New York Times* aviation reporter observed. C. R. Smith, the president of American Airlines, said the jetliner obviously had huge potential but that it was "much further in the future" than most people thought.

Some U.S. experts sensed complacency, and predicted that airline executives would soon come to regret it. Albert Douglas, a transport and naval torpedo pilot, writing in the March 1950 issue of *Harper's* magazine, imagined a scene at Idlewild Airport in 1953. At Gate 2 would be a new long-range British de Havilland Comet jet; at Gate 3, one of the long-range propeller planes used by U.S. carriers.

"If you are by then the president of an American airline and happen to be standing at Gate Two or Three," wrote Douglas, "the chances are you will be boiling mad, for the British plane will be packed and yours will be almost empty. If you are an American aircraft manufacturer you will recall nostalgically the good old days of 1949, when piston-engine American transports were the envy and the standard of the world's airlines—the fastest, the safest, and the most efficient to operate. Fantastic? Probably not. For jet transportation is here today. The British do have an acceptable jet transport." That, of course, was the de

Havilland Comet, then still in testing stage, but already pledged by BOAC to be ready within a year or two for the new jet "Empire" service.

"To most air-minded Americans the news of the British jet transport came as a shock," wrote Douglas, "for the experts have been telling them—and still are telling them, for that matter—that a ticket on a jet plane to London, or Podunk, is fifteen years away."

This was true as far as the airlines were concerned, and many in the aircraft industry did not see a need to rush into the Jet Age, either. In a speech in October 1952, Frederick B. Rentschler, a hugely talented engineer and chairman of the board of United Aircraft Corporation, the Boeing spin-off from the 1934 split of the company and one of the leading jet engine manufacturers, sounded unconcerned about the de Havilland Comet. The commercial jet age, he predicted, would not really dawn until the early 1960s.

Still, whatever the public pronouncements from the industry, Douglas (no apparent relation to the owner of the aircraft company) picked up private rumblings of frustration. "What appalled American aviation men the most was that our famous aircraft industry, which for two decades had led the world in transport aviation, did not have a working or prototype model of a jet in the air," Douglas reported. "A minority of the engineers went so far as to discount the British jet plane as 'before its time.' But the majority privately agreed with one airline president who made no bones about the matter. 'We've been caught short,' he said, 'and it's damned embarrassing.'"

Frankly, it was also somewhat humiliating from the American point of view to even ask the British about their jet transport work. "These were of the clan once considered here in America to be five years behind the times," noted Douglas. "Today they puff their pipes and cheerily evade questions about advanced British design."

One of several things going on at this point behind the scenes was a debate over funding. Many top executives, in both the airline and aircraft manufacturing business, did not believe that an effective jetliner could be developed without massive government funding. (This was much the same argument made a decade or so later about supersonic air transports.) At first, Boeing was firmly in this camp. "Government financial aid will be required if we are to overtake and pass the subsidized British aircraft industry in its bid for domination of the future jet transport field," an article in Boeing's employee magazine declared in 1949. "No company can risk its capital in the building of a wholly new type of airplane, such as the jet transport."

Allen lobbied the industry as well as the government. "We tried and we tried and we tried," he recalled. The Civil Aeronautics Board, a government agency, seemed prepared to sign on to the famous "No bucks, no Buck Rogers" philosophy, and announced backing for a plan that would provide a government subsidy of up to 75 percent for a commercial jet design. *The Washington Post*, in a 1952 editorial, said it would be a "misfortune if the American interest in civilian aircraft manufacture were allowed to atrophy. That can easily happen unless United States airlines pool their ideas and requirements and get together with manufacturers on prototypes of jet transports they will be able to afford." But the bill went nowhere in Congress. The Pentagon objected to civilian jetliner development because "such a move might interfere with military aircraft production," the United Press reported in May 1952.

"U.S. aircraft builders, busy with military jet orders, have made few moves to catch up with Britain's lead in jet transport," *Time* reported a few months later. "A few, like Douglas and Lockheed, have talked of blueprinting a model. But most have hopefully waited for a Government subsidy which never came, and for some real interest from the airlines."

But no airline was willing to stick its neck out to buy something that might not work in the marketplace, and apparently no U.S. air manufacturer was willing to build one without some commitment from the airlines.

"I went all over the world," Jack Steiner, a legendary Boeing engineer, recalled in a 1957 company symposium about the evolution of the 707 design. "Europe and the United States, to [all] the major airlines in the early part of 1950, attempting with our sales department to sell our Model 473. We found great interest, some statements that [in] another year they would buy, and so forth, but no cold cash. It involved millions of dollars and you almost stake the future of an airline on it, and there were no volunteers for that sort of money. . . . The airlines did not yet see the light strongly enough to invest." (Steiner, who was also a driving force behind the company's 727 and 737 jet aircraft, passed away in 2003 at the age of eighty-five.)

It was a chicken-or-egg dilemma, so even as the United States blasted full speed ahead with military jets, pushed on by the growing Cold War with the Soviets, nothing was done about a jet airliner. Great Britain, of course, had no such reservations.

Late in December 1942, some two and a half years before the war would actually end, a Conservative member of the British Parliament named W. R. D. Perkins rose to give a speech—not about the war, but about postwar aviation.

"I foresee that, as soon as the armistice comes, there will be a race between the Americans and ourselves to control the air lines of the world," Perkins warned his colleagues. The British government, he said, must settle with the American government at once which "spheres of influence" would belong to each country.

"Otherwise," Perkins thundered, "there will be friction. We might even have another Boston Tea Party."

While it seems odd in retrospect that a lawmaker would put a matter of civil competition in such contentious terms, especially when his nation was in a life or death struggle with Nazi Germany, he was far from the only person worried about peacetime friction in the skies. After all, nations had gone to war over control of the high seas and of trade across the oceans; what guarantees were there that bickering over the sky would not lead to battle?

Henry A. Wallace, Roosevelt's third-term vice president (he was let go in 1944 in favor of a Missouri senator, Harry Truman), foresaw an "air arm" of the future United Nations that might provide international air service, as did Sir Osborne Mance, in a 1943 survey of British aviation. "It is perhaps not too much to contemplate," Mance wrote, "that the international organization necessary for any form of international control on grounds of security should own or participate in the principal air services, and license all other air service."

Others argued for smaller groups of nations to come together to forge or oversee new cooperational airlines, harking back to a famous warning from Alfred Instone, a pioneer in the British aviation business, who just after World War I said: "It is impossible to control the air services of Europe on nationalist lines. You cannot have nearly forty sovereign countries each trying to wreck the air services of the other thirty-nine. Europe must be one area for air transport under one control, or there can be nothing but a few ferry services in operation."

Pan Am's leader, Juan Trippe, dismissed the co-op ideas as "wooly-headed internationalism," and Claire Booth Luce, the conservative journalist and Connecticut congresswoman, called it "globaloney."

Still, there was an emerging recognition that a new era of international travel was coming, and that some greater international framework would be needed to give airlines of one nation the rights to fly in or over other nations. "The modern airplane creates a new geographical dimension," Wendell Willkie, the Republican leader and 1940 presidential candidate, put it memorably in 1943. "A navigable ocean of air blankets the whole surface of the globe. There are no distant places any longer: the world is small and the world is one. The American people must grasp these new realities if they are to play their essential part in winning the war and building a world of peace and freedom."

Roosevelt and Churchill agreed that an international conference at the end of the war could hammer out such an agreement. Adolf Berle, a seasoned diplomat in charge of aviation matters in the State Department, said such a pact could help avoid a free-for-all in the skies. "In the air there is no excuse for an attempt to revive the sixteenth- and seventeenth-century conceptions," he wrote, "for a modern British East India Company or Portuguese trading monopoly or 'Spanish Main conception.'"

Intriguingly, however, British leaders began to have a conception of the air that was not altogether different from the one that had enabled them to master the seas. Parliament appointed a panel known as the Brabazon Committee, led by the pioneering aviator Lord Brabazon, to recommend some types of civilian airliners that British companies might build and sell to the world after the war. These deliberations led to the decision to go for it as far as a jet airliner was concerned. Since BOAC was a state-backed airline and the government held stakes in many of the manufacturers, there was no great debate about the role of the marketplace in deciding when and whether to build a jet. BOAC would order up a whole fleet of them straight off the drawing boards, and envious competitors would follow suit, so that was that. A product and a customer!

The British were convinced they could generate a worldwide market for the jetliner, and that the time was now. Whitney Straight, BOAC's managing director, conceded it was a risky step: "We took a gamble ordering Comets straight off the drawing board," he said. A top de Havilland official, C. T. Wilkins, put it this way: "Timing is a vital factor in producing a new aircraft and it is often better to produce a slightly inferior aircraft at the right time than a perfect one at the wrong time." Both statements would come to haunt the de Havilland company, and indeed the entire British aviation industry.

As the Brabazon panel drew up some specifications based on the most optimistic projections from the engineers about just how many passengers a first-generation jetliner could hold, BOAC itself was planning for its big role in the postwar world. It drew up something internally known as the Blue Book, a guide to restoring international aviation in peacetime—and, lo and behold, London was at the very center of it all.

"In planning future international organisation," declared the guide, "it is essential that London be recognised as the principal terminus of Atlantic and Commonwealth Empire routes and the gateway to Europe, and consequently as the appropriate seat for the controlling and regulating air authority."

In other words, as a publicity director for BOAC put it: "Great Britain will become an aeronautical Clapham Junction astride the most important air route of the future."

This was hubris, and the Americans would not accept it: the new authority, to be known as the International Air Transport Association, or IATA, wound up with twin head offices, one in Montreal, the other in Geneva. There was another row looming. If Pan Am had a "blue route" spanning the globe to start up shortly after the war, BOAC would have a "red route" linking British Commonwealth sites around the world. Churchill and

Roosevelt began to quarrel about the matter even before their common foes had declared surrender. The British prime minister hit the roof when he heard that Pan Am and the Irish were conducting a big negotiation over reciprocal landing rights. "Everyone here is astonished that this should have been started without our being told beforehand," he wrote to the president. FDR was no less testy, and more than a tad patronizing, in response. "I think it only fair to tell you," he told Churchill, "that aviation circles in this country are becoming increasingly suspicious that certain elements in England intend to try to block the development of international flying in general until the British aviation industry is further developed."

IATA, the new regulating authority, created in April 1945 at a conference in Havana, Cuba, did indeed manage to head off major skirmishes in the sky, unless one counts the "great sandwich war" of 1954, a reflection of the comical lengths to which the organization was forced to micromanage nearly every aspect of global air travel. With delegates holding up paddles to vote on fares and routes, it functioned as a sort of micro version of the United Nations—in fact, one of its director-generals, Knut Hammarskjöld, happened to be a nephew of the UN's first secretary-general, Dag Hammarskjöld.

In the complicated, absurdist structure of the IATA, international airlines agreed that passengers in tourist class would have to pay extra for onboard meals. But one day SAS, the Scandinavian carrier, started serving *smørrebrød*, the open-faced Danish version of a sandwich, and decided not to charge anything on the theory that *smørrebrød* was more of a snack than a meal.

American carriers complained, and the dispute escalated to the point that the United States threatened to withdraw SAS's landing rights in the country. SAS paid a $16,000 fine and lapped up the extensive international media coverage, and the issue was ultimately settled more or less in its favor, though IATA regulators decreed that one corner of the sandwich had to be visible—not covered by any spread—in order for it to be counted as a snack.

There were plenty of other disputes, and Umberto Nordio, the colorful head of Alitalia who had once been a shipping magnate, memorably declared: "I first hoisted my sails in a world of seafaring crooks, and now I spread my wings in a world of airborne crooks." Ted Wyman, an aide to Juan Trippe, once told Charles Lindbergh that international air negotiations were a form of torture. "The whole thing reminds me of an electric fan," Wyman said. "Anyone who sticks his fingers in it is going to get them cut off."

In reality, the situation was not so bad for Pan American World Airways. In fact, the airline was broadly referred to as the "chosen instrument" of U.S. international air policy, because it was often the carrier that secured a monopoly for the U.S. half of the given number of flights that the IATA allowed between two nations, or what Bin Cheng, a British professor of aviation law, called it, the "vast cobweb of bilateral national agreements" that governed air travel in the decades following the war.

So it was that many of Trippe's battles played out in Congress or the White House, where he had an especially tenuous relationship with FDR. Roosevelt once called Trippe "the most fascinating Yale gangster I ever met"—he thought Trippe inflated the price of government transport costs—and briefly considered nationalizing Pan Am under cover of the wartime emergency.

Trippe retained an iron grip over the approval for rights to dozens of countries, though in many ways he met his match in Howard Hughes, who managed to crack open the European markets for TWA and engaged in a memorable showdown with Senator Owen Brewster of Maine, a key Trippe ally, in which Hughes transformed a putative investigation of his aircraft company into a melee over Pan Am's influence in the corridors of Washington.

In the 2004 motion-picture version of Hughes's life, *The Aviator*, Alec Baldwin did a marvelous job as the Juan Trippe character, the monopolistic foil to the more democratically inclined Hughes, played by Leonardo DiCaprio. Among other things, Baldwin caught Trippe's obsession with the globe, which he thought must become firmly fixed in the traveler's mind as the true, three-dimensional indication of how far it was from point A to point B, rather than the old, misleading wall map based on the 1569 cartographic system invented by the Flemish geographer Gerardus Mercator.

The Mercator projection was "now hopelessly misleading for visualizing long flights," British journalist Anthony Sampson explained in a 1984 book about the international airline cartels. "It not only distorted the poles and the equator; it encouraged a 'Eurocentric' view, laying out the world from west to east with the land mass of Europe and Asia in the middle. Only the globe—which had become Juan Trippe's personal symbol—could make sense of the air-routes," Sampson wrote.

Still, while Hollywood needed to simplify the plot line, one aspect of the Trippe portrayal in *The Aviator* was unfair. Much as he fought to win and keep control of Pan Am's international routes, he was a veritable populist in the context of the IATA. Trippe knew the Jet Age was coming, and he foresaw, more clearly than anyone else, how air travel would eventually become the province of the masses. As he once put it: "The true objective is to bring to the life of the average man those things which were once the privilege of the fortunate few." In 1945, he introduced a new tourist-class fare that cut the round-trip fare between New York and London by more than half, to $275. Hardly affordable to most people—about $3,200 in today's dollars—but that precipitated a row with the British, who actually closed UK airports for a while to Pan Am flights that carried travelers paying the new fare, forcing them to land in Shannon, Ireland, instead. Within a few years, however, tourist or economy fares were standard on most international airlines.

The British editor Harold Evans perhaps captured it best, in a rejoinder to the cinematic portrayal of Trippe that he wrote in *The Wall Street Journal* shortly after the movie came out. "If you are one of the 3.6 billion who have flown on a 747, it's Trippe, not Hughes, who merits the raising of a turbulence-free glass," wrote Evans. "The democratization he effected was as real as Henry Ford's."

Trippe was yet another "Winged Gospel" preacher—a believer

in peace through tourism, in sum—and some of his pronouncements now take on a sadly overoptimistic tone in light of the September 2001 attack on the World Trade Center towers (which
were originally designed to withstand the impact of a Boeing
707 without immediately collapsing—and did—but not the subsequent fire). "The tourist plane, if allowed to move forward
unshackled by political boundaries and economic restrictions,
will win this race between education and catastrophe," Trippe
told an IATA conference in 1955. "Mass travel by air may prove
to be more significant to world destiny than the atom bomb."

And others were beginning to see a new era of mass international tourism for Americans during the relatively prosperous
1950s. In early 1953, *Holiday* magazine asked one travel agent to
describe the new type of international traveler. "Thirty years
ago, I set up the grand tour for a wealthy widow and her el-
derly traveling companion," the agent said. "Fifteen years ago,
I made arrangements for businessmen, Hollywood stars" and a
few other denizens of high society. "Today, I deal with expense-
account wanderers, solid suburban citizens and schoolteachers.
Tomorrow, praise be, the office will be full of plumbers and their
babies."

By the time he gave his speech about mass travel trumping
the atom bomb, Juan Trippe was no longer dragging his heels
on a jet airliner: he was all-in on a gamble to make Pan Am
the preeminent jet carrier in the world. His archrival Howard
Hughes had entered the fray, obsessed with the notion of mak-

The Boeing 247, introduced in 1933. *The Boeing Company Collection at The Museum of Flight*

The Douglas DC-3, one of the most successful airliners ever built. *Flagship Detroit Foundation—Bonnie Kratz/EAA*

Ellen Church, the world's first airline stewardess. *United Airlines Creative Services*

"The Original Eight," all registered nurses. *© Boeing*

Stewardess service quickly became a key part of airline advertising. *United Airlines Creative Services*

A United stewardess on a Boeing 247. *The Museum of Flight*

Juan Trippe, the head of Pan Am, Boeing's lead customer for the 707. *The Museum of Flight*

Juan Trippe with Charles Lindbergh. *Pan American World Airways, courtesy The Museum of Flight*

The Messerschmitt Me 262, the world's first operational jet. *The National Museum of the United States Air Force*

Sir Frank Whittle, the British inventor of the jet engine. *Imperial War Museum*

Sir Geoffrey de
Havilland.
© BAE SYSTEMS

Captain John "Cat's
Eyes" Cunningham.
© BAE SYSTEMS

Cunningham
in the Comet
cockpit.
© BAE SYSTEMS

Cunningham in
front of the Comet,
under construction.
© BAE SYSTEMS

Test flight of
the Comet.
© BAE SYSTEMS

"Yoke Peter," the world's first jet airliner, leaving London Airport on its inaugural flight, May 1952. *British Airways Heritage Centre*

Comet and camels, on the plane's stopover at Khartoum, Sudan, during its inaugural run to Africa, 1952. *British Airways Heritage Centre*

ing TWA the first U.S. airline to fly jetliners. Suddenly, American, Eastern, and United were pounding on the door at Boeing, Lockheed, and Douglas, internal correspondence and phone transcripts show.

"Charley Froesch of Eastern called me to see if it would be possible for me to return to New York to go over our jet transport proposal," K. C. Gordon, Boeing's chief sales engineer, reported to Allen in October 1952, roughly the same time that Eastern's chief, Eddie Rickenbacker, was also talking to de Havilland about a massive order for new Comets.

Eastern, Gordon continued, was "extremely interested in our airplane. They have ideal routes for a jet transport." American's chief of sales pressed Gordon as well: "It is urgent that Boeing give us some indication regarding future plans for commercial [jet] production," he cabled Seattle in June 1953.

It was in many ways a clandestine affair, with the airlines privately disparaging one aircraft company to another and the aircraft companies pressing the airlines to show some fortitude by committing tens of millions of dollars to a particular jet model. It took on the air of negotiation over a wedding dowry. An Eastern sales chief "assured me that EAL was not married to Lockheed and that they were in a position to buy whatever equipment was deemed optimal for EAL requirements," his Boeing counterpart wrote to headquarters. "Petty assured me United was not married to Douglas and they were open-minded and would buy the airplane best suited to their requirements," was the Boeing man's internal summary of another set of conversations.

What in the world had changed? Why were airlines that had

put off any plans for jets now in a scramble with one another to be first out of the gate with them, at least among U.S. carriers? Why were aircraft manufacturers, who only a year before had pressed Congress for cooperative jet development funds, now pummeling each other with their own, separate designs?

One galvanizing force was obvious: the de Havilland Comet. Despite all the American skepticism, the Comet was in the flush of success in 1952. The British had done it, and they were reaping the prestige. There was a waiting list of a month or more on some jet Comet routes, and as far as the U.S. industry was concerned, the banter about orders, between de Havilland and airline titans such as Trippe and Rickenbacker, was a bucket of cold water in the face.

But there was another reason that the battle for jetliners was on in the United States. Despite the doubts, the pleas to Congress for development aid and the military's announced objection, one man had decided to jump on the path to the future—Bill Allen.

Allen had been debating the issue for months. He agonized over the risks of failure, which could ruin his company and all but shut off the lights in Seattle. He had gone around the table, not once but several times, with his team of engineers and salesmen, some of whom were adamantly against jumping into the civilian fray. With the Cold War on and the Pentagon eager for jet fighters and bombers, why risk it? On the other hand, to the proponents, the engineers just chomping at the bit to build and deliver a world-beating jetliner, Allen could occasionally turn petulant. "Christ, whose money are you spending?" Allen blurted at one meeting.

Actually, Bill Allen, the lawyer, had discovered something very interesting about the question of whose money the company would be spending. It seems counterintuitive that a confiscatory federal tax rate could spur any company to develop a major technological innovation, but this is exactly what happened. During the Korean War, Congress had put an "excess profits tax" in effect, intended to prevent military companies from making out too well because of increased demand during a war. As it happened, the law essentially defined "excess profits" as anything above what a company had made during the peacetime period of 1946 to 1949. For Boeing, of course, peace had been a sock to the pocketbook; it had hardly made anything in that time. Therefore, as orders ramped up for the war, Boeing stood to face the "excess profits" tax on virtually every dollar of its profit, while a company such as Douglas, which had had its hands full rolling out propeller-driven airliners after the war, wouldn't face the higher trigger until its military sales equaled the bonanza it had made on commercial sales.

At a blush, it all sounded like an unfair tax burden on Boeing, and Bill Allen might have gone hollering to Washington state's congressional delegation to rectify the situation. But Allen the tax lawyer looked at the numbers and saw a golden opportunity. It worked like this: Because nearly all of its 1951 war-related earnings were considered "excess," the Boeing company would wind up owing eighty-two cents of every dollar of profit to Uncle Sam. The effective rate would be even higher if it paid out the remaining money in shareholder dividends, since individuals would have to pay taxes on those distributions as well.

Douglas Aircraft's rate worked out to sixty-eight cents on the dollar; Lockheed's, only forty-eight cents.

What Bill Allen clearly saw was that now was the perfect time to plow a huge amount of company money into an audacious new development project. Why not? All of it would be a legitimate business expense, reducing the "profits" for the coming years, but so what? That was all money that would have basically gone to the government. As long as he could persuade the board that he was putting the company in a long-term position of leading the field with a jetliner, its members were unlikely to object. Yes, it was a huge gamble, but for every dollar of the dice roll, only eighteen cents of it would have been Boeing's money to keep anyway. For Douglas and Lockheed, both in a much lower tax bracket, that was not so easy a call.

"The exact instant had arrived for Boeing to make its move, and Allen was alert enough to snatch the opportunity," explained Eugene Rodgers, a management expert and author of a 1996 book about the Boeing company, *Flying High*. Federal tax policy, of all things, had helped the cautious, prudent Bill Allen to forge ahead with jetliner development. "This was a defining moment," Rodgers concluded, without exaggeration, "the decision that made the company what it is today."

Allen had seen the Comet, at an air show in Farnborough, England, in 1950, while it was still in production and testing, and his response was curiously evocative of the conversation back in 1914 between Bill Boeing and Conrad Westervelt, the one that had launched the company.

"I think we could build a better one!" Boeing had told Westervelt that day on Lake Washington.

At a dinner in London just after the air show, Bill Allen had a question for one of his top engineers, Maynard Pennell. "How do you like the Comet?" "We could do better," said Pennell. Allen thought about it some more, and even zipped himself up in a flight suit for a test of various military jets. He was impressed not only by the speed, but also by the lack of vibration and noise, compared with the rat-a-tat motion and roar of a propeller airliner.

Allen had yet another powerful reason for taking a chance on the jet airliner. He was feeling increasingly confident that Boeing would get the important military contract for a jet tanker—and the tanker was about the right size for a big new airliner as well. Why not aim at both targets with one airplane? Such was the genius of the Dash-80 prototype that indeed it could be pitched to both the Air Force and the airlines, for two entirely separate purposes.

One day in March 1952, Allen called the managerial staff in for a meeting. "I was in—you know, you've got the underlings that are in the back row," recalled Bob Withington, a young assistant at the time. "I was in the back row there, and I watched [and] listened to Bill Allen conduct that meeting." Allen went around the table and listened yet again.

"Bill just sat back and said, 'Well, I guess that's it,'" Withington recounted.

That *was* it. A month later Allen got the board's go-ahead, and he told his engineers to draw up some plans but keep it all quiet for a few more months. Then in the summer of 1952, the consummate lawyer issued the most carefully crafted of statements—complete with a suggestion, though not an explicit statement, that perhaps Boeing had been at work on the idea far longer than it really had been. "The Boeing Company," announced Bill Allen, "has for some time been engaged in a company-financed project which will enable it to demonstrate a prototype jet airplane of new design to the armed services and the commercial airlines in the summer of 1954."

Of all the words in Allen's sparse announcement, one was particularly important: "demonstrate." Boeing was developing a product that would shrink the world, but the airlines still weren't biting. It would need somebody to sell the airplane, a master showman, a politician, a first-class schmoozer, someone whose enthusiasm for what the company had to offer could push a sale across the finish line. Boeing had him, right in the cockpit.

five

Ambassadors to the Air

Tex Johnston

One Saturday in the spring of 1925, an eleven-year-old Kansas farm boy named Alvin Johnston listened closely as an unfamiliar buzzing sound grew louder and louder over Emporia, the little town where he lived. He ran to the south side of the house and looked up at the sky. "It's an airplane!" he shouted to his father. The plane banked in low toward the house, but then tilted up to the left, turned, and headed west. Johnston thought it would disappear, but suddenly the plane turned again, and headed downward.

"Dad!" shouted Alvin Johnston. "It's going to land!"

To which his father could only say: "Why would he land here?"

The plane indeed had landed, on a broad stretch of green pasture belonging to a neighbor. There were several horse-drawn buggies, wagons, and three Model Ts parked on a dirt road alongside the makeshift landing strip. The men wore bib overalls, the ladies wore long cotton dresses that reached nearly to their ankles. Other children milled about, and the pilot leaned on a fence, "his well-worn but beautiful English riding boot rest[ing] on a lower strand of barbed wire." He wore a soft brown leather jacket over a soldier's shirt with pockets on either side, and slightly flared English riding breeches with chamois knee patches. He had a brown leather helmet with the goggles pushed up, and a long white scarf looped around his neck. He stood a bit over six feet tall, with "a tapering black mustache, friendly blue eyes, and square jaw." He was patiently and cheerfully answering questions from the gathering crowd.

So Alvin "Tex" Johnston remembered it all, more than sixty-five years later.

Tex was a masterful storyteller with an encyclopedic eye and ear for recalling detail, or a great narrative imagination, or perhaps a bit of both. As vividly and colorfully as he recalled each and every aspect of the event, the point of his story was this: He got bitten by the flying bug that day, and the spell lasted for the rest of his long and eventful life.

The tall pilot was looking for passengers; he was selling sightseeing rides to finance his tiny propeller plane. But as curious as everyone was, no one volunteered for the thrill, and the pilot began walking toward the plane with a friendly farewell. Suddenly a voice came from the crowd.

"Come on, Dad, let's go," Tex recalled imploring his father. "Please, Dad, let me go. Ask the pilot if I can go."

Johnston's father hesitated a bit, and the pilot kept on walking.

"Hey, mister," he suddenly called at the pilot. "Can the boy go?"

The pilot turned and looked back at Alvin, who said he stood as tall as his eleven-year-old frame could possibly let him.

"Please, mister, I just have to fly."

The pilot looked at the boy's father and asked, "Don't you want to come along?"

"No, I guess not," said the father. "But the boy wants to go."

So the pilot took the boy by the hand and as they walked to the small plane, he told Tex: "It'll be a little noisy and a little breezy."

The pilot lifted the boy into the front cockpit, and strapped a safety cord around him. The boy was so short, he recalled, that he couldn't see over the side, and so he wriggled upward under the belt, and got on his knees. Now he could see.

The pilot walked around the wing to the propeller, and yanked to give it a start. "Engine noise, prop wash, and vibration all started up together," recalled Johnston. As the pilot slid into the rear cockpit, he winked a clear blue eye at the boy. He eased the plane toward a takeoff heading.

"The throb of the engine increased to a roar, the slipstream became a constant rush, the irregular bumping of the wheels over the uneven ground smoothed out and ceased completely as the cockpit seat tilted upward," Tex Johnston recalled. "I peered over the edge of the cockpit. The ground fell away. We were flying!"

It was only a few minutes in the air, but Johnston could recall it all vividly—white houses, red barns, the Neosho River, the little town of Emporia "looking about the size of the top of my school desk."

Soon the plane came to a bumpy landing and rolled back toward the fence, where Johnston saw his townspeople, waving and laughing and pointing. When the propeller stopped, Alvin Johnston leapt to the ground, grabbed the pilot's hand, and proclaimed: "I love you and I'm going to be just like you!"

"I believe you liked it," said his father, smiling happily. The younger Johnston waxed enthusiastic: "Please go for a ride," he told the people of his town. "It's wonderful!" So he set out on the path to becoming a pilot, but he was already a salesman for the air. And as he climbed into his father's car, he could still hear the pilot's booming voice: "Come on, folks! See your hometown from the air! Only one dollar!"

Back at home, Alvin lay on warm grass that was dotted with Kansas dogtooth violets, and looked at white puffball clouds. He wanted to get back into the sky.

The boy wrote away for airplane pictures, and he got them, from the Waco Airplane Company in Troy, Ohio; the Travel Air company in Wichita; American Eagle in Kansas City; Monocoupe in St. Louis. He bought aviation magazines and studied the names of the components of a plane: fuselage, ailerons, stabilizers, rudders, elevators. To him they were magic words.

At fifteen, he took "a first step in financing my dreams." He began delivering the daily Kansas City newspapers. The subscriber's monthly cost was sixty-five cents, of which Tex had to pay forty-five cents to the district agent. Soon he was netting thirty dollars a month. One day a man named Toy Franklin flew into town in a Waco model, a three-place open-cockpit biplane. Alvin Johnston was taking flying lessons.

Toy offered the student some advice. "Never think of moving the rudder, ailerons, or elevators. Think in terms of pressure: right and left pressure on the rudder pedals for directional control, side pressure on the stick for a roll, and fore-and-aft pressure on the stick to move the nose upwards toward you or away from you. Don't think of nose up and nose down.

"That way," concluded Toy, "when you advance to acrobatics and get on your back, you won't be confused." Johnston was already getting a taste of stunt flying.

He started moving up in the Kansas aviation world. One Saturday morning, an unfamiliar-sounding high-wing monoplane circled over the grassy airstrip at Emporia and lumbered in for a landing. The plane rolled toward Johnston, the prop ticked to a stop, and out stepped the first female pilot he had ever seen.

"I'm Al Johnston," he said, sticking out his hand. "My name's Amelia," she said. During lunch at the Coney Island Café on Sixth Avenue in Emporia, the two traded stories of flight. The woman said her last name was Earhart, and she said she was trying to accumulate hours on a prototype engine, which, Johnston later recalled, explained why the engine sound was new to him.

"The Earhart name had no significance for me at the time," Johnston wrote decades later in his autobiography, *Tex Johnston: Jet-Age Test Pilot.* She "was not beautiful, but her easy conversation and pleasing, radiant personality made a deep impression." Then he put the meeting in classic Tex terms. "The two hours we spent together was the only time our flight plans in life intersected. Later, seeing her name in headlines, I thought of our chance meeting at Maddock's pasture."

Soon Tex was working for Art Inman's Flying Circus; not as a pilot at first, but as an energetic advance man, a grease monkey, and an on-site guard who slept next to the planes at night. He honed his sales skills.

"Airplanes were considered somewhat miraculous," Johnston recalled, "and many people were afraid of them. So during barnstorming days it was always difficult to sell the first tickets. In fact, if one could persuade someone to go for a free ride, it was well worth the effort and the cost, particularly if the first passenger was enthusiastic after landing."

Johnston took an airplane mechanics course at the Spartan school in Tulsa, learning the craft from a nationally known expert, Vance Vassacheck. Soon he had enough money to enroll in a commercial pilot's course and in 1933, he said, "a revolutionary new transport airplane indirectly widened my horizons still farther." That was the Boeing 247, the plane that launched a new era of air travel. When the plane reached Tulsa one day on a demonstration tour, Johnston was thrilled. A short while later, he met Will Rogers, the legendary humorist and a fervent airplane evangelist.

When he met with Johnston and other flight students in 1933, Rogers was deeply enthusiastic. "I hear you've been flying all over Oklahoma and Kansas," he said. "The airplane has a great future, and this country needs good pilots like you boys." Rogers remained a flight advocate until the day he perished—in an airplane crash that also took the life of aviation legend Wiley Post, near Barrow, Alaska, in August 1935.

Johnston was now an aircraft mechanic and a pilot, the proud owner of limited commercial pilot's license number 29948. He returned to Inman's barnstorming outfit, and now he was flying the planes, but it was a tough sled. The Depression was at its peak. "It was disheartening to watch people with their faces grim from worry, their clothing threadbare, meticulously counting the change in their pockets to come up with a dollar for an airplane ride," Johnston recalled in his autobiography. "But their eyes were bright with the anticipation of flying—a bit of joy, if only for a few minutes. Throughout my barnstorming days I cannot recall a passenger's ever saying he or she did not enjoy the experience."

When Johnston was a sophomore in high school, he had dated DeLores Honea, whom he described as "an attractive blond from Emporia." He ran into her at a party during one of his trips home, and the fire was rekindled, and in June 1935 they were married. There wasn't enough money to be made in barnstorming, so to supplement his pilot's income, the couple became motion-picture screeners, running the small Rialto Theater in Lyndon, Kansas, followed by a stint at the fourteen-hundred-seat New Bays Theater in Blackwell, Oklahoma.

By selling the smaller theater, Tex and DeLores were able to finance a move to Manhattan—Manhattan, Kansas, that is, where Tex could begin to take some classes toward a college degree at Kansas State University in the late 1930s. But he was worried that his piloting career was running into a bit of a stall.

That concern, however, evaporated as the country moved closer toward possible involvement in World War II: quickly, Tex Johnston's skills were very much in demand.

On the day he read of the Roosevelt administration's Civilian Pilot Training program, he cut class and headed for the airport. He never did get his Kansas State degree. At the Manhattan airport he found a Pan American captain, Frank Selken, from Miami, organizing a new flight school in a dilapidated hangar made of corrugated metal. "I understand you need a flight instructor," said Johnston, laying his flying license and his pilot's logbook on Selken's desk.

Soon Tex had a flight instructor rating and a full-time job, as well as an appreciation for how profoundly the world—his world—had changed in eastern Kansas. "On a south takeoff I could see the foundations of the old World War I Camp Funston, where 22 years before I had shivered in the frozen ruts of the dirt road in 10-degree weather while Dad talked through a wire fence with his brother, my uncle Frank, quarantined by the flu epidemic," he recalled. He could never forget the row upon row of dead bodies, frozen stiff, waiting for burial once the ground thawed. "As I flew over that area, I considered the progress since that day when Mother had waited in a side-curtained Model T touring car with a quilt over her feet and legs that retained the feeble heat of a kerosene lantern. The roads were frozen mud, 90 percent of the vehicles were horse-drawn, and there was no electricity or running water or indoor facilities. [Now] here I was flying over the same area at 90 mph in a closed-cockpit airplane warmed by a cabin heater. The roads were now paved, not a single horse-drawn vehicle could be seen, and electricity, hot and cold running water, and indoor facilities were standard—all accomplished in roughly twenty years. Looking ahead, I believed that the coming war would spark research and development at an even faster rate, a rate never before experienced. Here I sat in the cockpit of an airplane at 2,000 feet, a first meager step into that future."

Tex entered the war as an instructor in Texas, then as a pilot in the U.S. Army Air Corps Ferry Command. In December 1942, with the United States now fully engaged in the war, he became a test pilot. He was sent to Bell Aircraft, in Niagara Falls, New York, where he worked with engineers to improve the P-39 "Airacobra," one of the main fighter aircraft in the U.S. fleet, and to develop the XP-59A "Airacomet," the first American jet fighter, which was built toward the end of the war and was an important forerunner in U.S. military jet development though it saw no service in the conflict. His services were so in demand at the design stage that he never got sent overseas during the war—for him, not a source of relief, but of frustration. After the war he took a turn developing the Bell helicopter, and moved to Houston to help sell the company's choppers to oil and exploration companies across Texas and Louisiana.

In his travels around the country, there didn't seem to be a part of it that Tex didn't love—his native Kansas; rural Texas, where the turkey, deer, and dove hunting were the best; upstate New York, which had spectacular beauty; California's Mojave Desert, where he traded flying notes with Chuck Yeager and one day in October 1944 found himself at 46,000 feet on a high-speed jet run heading for the Pacific Ocean, in the cockpit of an XP-59A. "I felt a source of joy and exhilaration," he said. "Here I am in one of the most advanced airplanes in the world, flying in a totally new environment." And, he said to himself, "I'm the only person in the United States up here!"

One day in 1948, Johnston found himself a passenger aboard a Boeing-built Stratocruiser, descending over the Cascade Mountains toward Seattle. He looked out the window and saw the sparkling, snowy crests of Mounts Rainier and St. Helens (long before the latter blew her top), and below him magnificent green stretches of forest. For all the other places he'd lived in and loved, "this was my kind of country. As it turned out, the Pacific Northwest became my favorite area of the world and, thanks to the Invisible Hand, our home."

He was impressed right away by the obvious fondness and pride the taxi driver felt for Seattle. "In his opinion," Tex recalled, "Seattle was a Boeing town, the weather ideal, no violent temperature variations, a boater's paradise, excellent fishing and hunting, and, of course the University of Washington." Johnston told the man he would recommend him to the local chamber of commerce, but the driver squinted an eye and as he drove away called, "Thanks! I'm happy on the street."

Johnston was on his way to an interview with the Boeing Airplane Company, where he would soon become a test pilot for both the B-47 Stratojet and the forthcoming B-52 Stratofortress, an eight-engine jet behemoth that would be able to fly halfway around the world without refueling. Barely a year into his new job, the dangers of the occupation got brought home in a most tragic way to Johnston and the other test pilots. One of their colleagues, E. Scott Osler, a former Pan American pilot, was killed when the bubble-shaped canopy of a Boeing XB-47 Stratojet sheared off its moorings in flight and struck him in the head. His copilot managed to get the jet plane down for an emergency landing, but Osler was already dead.

While Johnston started out at Boeing as a pilot of military jets, he would become the chief test pilot for its commercial ventures. And in a forty-two-year career in aviation, he would be best known as the test pilot for Boeing's first jet airliner—and for what he had done with the prototype Dash-80 on that day of the hydroplane races in 1955, his famous barrel roll.

As Boeing began lining up the heads of airlines to come to Seattle and see the future of air travel, Tex Johnston would turn out to be a perfect ambassador to the air, selling these executives and their chief pilots on the Boeing 707 and his "college of jet knowledge" with his unflagging enthusiasm. He frequently invited his visitors to take the captain's seat, though he could keep ultimate command with an identical set of controls in the copilot's seat.

Bill Cook, a Boeing engineer in charge of the high-speed wind tunnel, said Tex Johnston was "a master" during this sales demonstration, especially when a fellow pilot was involved. "The airline pilot would be very much elated, as it was his first exposure to high altitude cruise above the weather," Cook recalled. "He would have noted the lack of vibration, the low cockpit noise, and the ease of control. This was a sales opportunity never again to be equaled on account of the dramatic nature of the transition from piston engines and propellers to jets." The airplane was impressive enough on its own, Cook said with a chuckle, "but having Tex in there did help to seal the deal. He had sort of a contagious enthusiasm, if you will. That guy was a born showman."

Johnston's counterpart at the de Havilland company, Group Captain John "Cat's Eyes" Cunningham, was a deft salesman as well, though in a much more understated, British way. No one could possibly imagine the shy, proper Cunningham ever barrel-rolling the de Havilland Comet. While Alvin Johnston reveled in a nickname, "Tex," that was based on a myth (the idea that he was from Texas), "Cat's Eyes" Cunningham was embarrassed by his, also based on a fib. His wartime jet-fighting skills, he insisted to anyone who would listen, had far more to do with engineering and radar improvements than to any special powers in his eyes. And while the British newspapers lapped it up when a military spokesman said with a straight face that "Cat's Eyes" Cunningham was so good because he ate carrots by the bunchful, Cunningham would explain—after the war, anyway—that the explanation was "rubbish."

However sharp his vision, "Cat's Eyes" did bring another skill to his nocturnal battles with Nazi bombers, twenty of which he shot down during the war. "Cunningham was able to think in three dimensions, an extremely useful ability when flying at night," explained Brian Marshall, whose Rapid Pictures film production company interviewed Cunningham for a documentary called *Boffins, Beams and Bombs.* The pilot "thought out his strategy just like a chess match." Furthermore, as Mike Ramsden explained it in a pamphlet about Cunningham prepared for the de Havilland Aircraft Heritage Centre in Hertfordshire, perhaps the "Cat's Eyes" legend was not a total myth.

"Climbing a Comet through cloud one day and br[e]aking into dazzling sunshine, he said, 'There's an Ambassador,' before others on the flight deck could even spot a distant speck," recalled Ramsden. "He knew England from the air like the back of his hand, usually identifying a landmark immediately on breaking cloudbase."

It was John Cunningham who was at the controls early on the evening of July 27, 1949, when Comet G-ALVG, or Victor George, shot down the runway with a piercing scream. Though it would not be considered the first jetliner—that honor would belong to "Yoke Peter," which three years later would be the first to carry passengers in scheduled service—it was the first such aircraft aloft on a test flight. "The world changed as our wheels left the runway," said the flight test observer, Tony Fairbrother.

With Hollywood-quality good looks and a futuristic jetliner to show off, Cunningham cut a dashing figure around the world, setting speed records and drawing orders not only from Britain, but also from France, Canada, and, perhaps most triumphantly, from the titan of Pan Am, Juan Trippe. A lifelong bachelor, Cunningham would turn aside reporters' questions about his romantic interests by pointing to the Comet and saying: "That's my wife. She's beautiful and drinks paraffin."

While the two test pilots, Cunningham and Johnston, were up front selling their jetliners to the executives, they were far from the only ones selling the excitement of jet travel to the general public. In fact, in addition to the pilots, called "captains" and dressed in uniforms with winged epaulets that gave them an important psychological aura of authority and competence, each airline would wind up with several more uniformed representatives on any given flight, and these young diplomats were even more visible, since they shared the main cabin with the customers themselves. They were iconic to the Jet Age, lending an aura of charm and cheer to air travel, and they just happened to have their origin in a marketing brainstorm dreamed up by the Boeing Airplane Company.

One day toward the end of February 1930, Steve Stimpson, the traffic agent in the San Francisco division of an airline known as the Boeing Air Transport Company, fired off a cable to his superiors in Seattle. "It strikes me that there would be a great psychological punch to having young women stewardesses or couriers, or whatever you want to call them" aboard Boeing's small airplanes, wrote Stimpson. "Imagine the national publicity we could get from it, and the tremendous effect it would have on the traveling public."

Stimpson had a very particular sort of young woman in mind for the task. She would be good at soothing nervous passengers in commercial flight, an enterprise that was still very much associated with great danger by the public. Not without reason: of the forty original pilots hired by the Post Office Department in 1918 to launch the civil aviation system in the United States, thirty-one had been killed in air crashes over the subsequent decade. If today's airline passengers were subjected to 1929 air crash rates, seven thousand of them would die every year in the United States alone.

This new stewardess, Stimpson reasoned, would be of help and console in the all-too-common events of air sickness, frayed nerves, or an emergency landing. The perfect candidate, he said, would be a registered nurse.

"I am not suggesting at all the flapper type of girl," he reassured the head office. "The average graduate nurse is a girl with some horse sense and is very practical and has seen enough of men to not be inclined to chase them around the block at every opportunity." Further, he said, all but with a locker-room wink stenciled on the cable, "as a general rule nurses are not of the 'pretty' type which lends to their usefulness in this situation."

Stimpson's proposal was met immediately with a one-word telegram of response: "No!"

As it happened, the idea did not actually originate with Stimpson, but with a twenty-five-year-old woman from an Iowa farm town named Ellen Church, who dreamed of an opportunity to fly. What Church really wanted to do was to pilot the airplane, and she had even spent some of her savings taking fly-ing lessons. But in the thinking of the age, no airline executive in his right mind would let someone with the temperament and fortitude—the flightiness—of a *woman* be in charge of an air-liner. Church, a University of Minnesota–trained nurse living in San Francisco, had been window-shopping one day when she noticed an office sign for Boeing's air service. She and Stimpson struck up a friendship, and soon Church was talking up the next best alternative to being a pilot. She could, she told him, be an excellent flight attendant, and she could find plenty of other nurses who would be, too.

"Mr. Stimpson," Church recalled telling him, "if women were casually living in the air, choosing to work there, wouldn't it have a good psychological effect and help rid the public of any fear?" Stimpson agreed, enthusiastically, and didn't take his first no from Seattle for a final answer.

Only in the past few years had the need for employing any sort of on-board attendants even crossed airline executives' minds. In fact, the U.S. airline system was originally conceived without passengers in mind at all. It was designed to carry the mail.

In an age when we are all used to transmitting and re-ceiving instant electronic mail, and refer somewhat derisively to the actual letters and packages we send to one another as "snail mail," it is perhaps difficult to appreciate what a revolutionary concept "air mail" was when the federal Post Office Department launched the service one day in 1918.

Moreover, Church's "stewardess" idea and Stimpson's fer-vent promotion of it came in the context of a marked polarity in the way that the potential traveling public saw the very concept of air travel: with tremendous fascination and sheer terror.

In many ways, the reality of powered, heavier-than-air flight, achieved by the Wright brothers at Kitty Hawk in December 1903, first generated a remarkable optimism. The airplane, its inventors and its many proponents believed, would do nothing less than bring a lasting peace to mankind.

"We thought we were introducing into the world an invention which would make further wars practically impossible," said Orville Wright himself. Shortly after Blériot, the Frenchman, made his famous flight across the English Channel, *The Independent* of London said the airplane would be a powerful force for good because it "creates propinquity, and propinquity begats love rather than hate."

Across the pond, similar soaring thoughts were expressed as part of what historian Joseph Corn rightly calls the Winged Gospel. Republican Philander C. Knox, the secretary of state under President William Howard Taft, said airplanes would "bring the nations much closer together and in that way eliminate war." Charlotte Perkins Gilman, a sociologist and early feminist theorist, drew a distinction between "earthy man" of all previous generations and the new man to whom flight was no longer an imaginary longing. "Aerial man as opposed to earthy man cannot think of himself further as a worm of the dust," wrote Gilman, "but [only] as a butterfly, psyche, the risen soul."

As it happened, the airplane was hardly an unalloyed force for good. Not two years after Blériot's famous crossing, the Italian military used an airplane to drop a grenade on a Turkish encampment in Libya, and within two years, several other European nations were experimenting with aerial warfare. As is often the case with technology, war spurred quantum leaps in aeronautical knowledge, and soon enough, with a world war raging, British Aces and German Flying Barons were dropping bombs and engaging in dogfights. Barely twenty years after the end of that war came a second world war, in which airplanes were used on both sides to cause unprecedented devastation with bombings of civilian populations and, for the first and only time in history, nuclear bombs were dropped from the sky on two large cities, Hiroshima and Nagasaki.

Though it was drawn relatively late into World War I, the United States Army (then in charge of air forces) managed to crank out hundreds of single-engine propeller-driven airplanes from a de Havilland design for the cause and train the pilots to fly them, thus enabling the Post Office to shift the armada to peaceful causes just as soon as the war was over. This was the beginning of air mail, and one customer group above all others was eager to see the new service spread as rapidly as possible: banks.

The banking industry quickly realized that air mail could slash the float time for checks and other financial documents (time is money, after all), and it wasted no time in pressing Congress not only for routes across the country, but for cheaper rates as well. Air mail actually turned a profit for the government in its first year of service, bringing in $162,000 on expenses of $143,000, and many people thought it reasonable for banks and others to pay the premium involved—twenty-four cents per ounce, about $3.50 in today's money—for the faster air service.

But 1918 was to be the one and only year the post office ever made any money whatsoever on air mail. Within a year, under heavy lobbying of Congress and the Post Office by the financial industry, air-mail rates were slashed: to sixteen cents per ounce, then six cents, and finally, on July 19, to zero.

This was crazy, for it provided no dedicated stream of revenue to build up a safe air system, with better avionics in the planes and critical safety measures on the ground such as lights on the runways and navigational beacons along the air routes. Furthermore, the pay-for-delivery structure put tremendous pressure on the pilots to fly no matter what the weather, one of several reasons that being an air-mail pilot proved to be such a fantastically dangerous profession in these early years of air mail. Half the forty pilots first hired were dead in crashes by the end of 1920, and half of the remaining half would die the same way in the coming years.

Slowly, some sanity was restored to the system, new air-mail rates put in effect, and routes put up for bid by private carriers. By 1927, the year that Charles Lindbergh captivated the world with his nonstop flight from New York to Paris, networks of small carriers were flying sacks of mail across the country. On average, they were indeed zippier than trains, but still far from breakneck speed: the transcontinental route from New York to San Francisco, for instance, had to stop for refueling at least once in Pennsylvania, twice in Ohio, once in Illinois, once in Iowa, twice in Nebraska, three times in Wyoming, once in Utah, and twice in Nevada.

Lindbergh's epic journey in *The Spirit of St. Louis,* lasting thirty-three and a half hours and covering 3,610 miles, made the twenty-five-year-old aviator an instant sensation, a worldwide celebrity, and fired people's imaginations about the possibilities of air travel.

"Lindbergh is no ordinary man," wrote the *Sunday Express* of London. "His daring dazzles the world. It is difficult to imagine anything more desperately heroic than his solitary flight across the ocean." Harold M. Anderson of the New York *Sun* took the theme of solo flight and turned it on itself. "Alone?" Anderson wrote. "Is he alone at whose right side rides Courage, with Skill within the cockpit and Faith upon the left? Does solitude surround the brave when Adventure leads the way and Ambition reads the dials? Is there no company with him for whom the air is cleft by Daring and the darkness is made light by Emprise?" For such "emprise"—a word meaning knightly daring or prowess—Lindbergh was selected as *Time* magazine's very first Man of the Year.

Lucky Lindy himself was a most willing apostle of the Winged Gospel. It was not just that airplanes could at last bring "the eyes of birds to the minds of men," as he put it. Lindbergh believed they could be a force for peace. "The thing that interests me now," the young aviator told his wife, Anne Morrow Lindbergh, "is breaking up the prejudices between nations, linking them up through aviation."

Bit by bit, the air travel system became safer, the planes larger, the times quicker. As that happened, it was entirely natural for airlines to begin offering space on their planes to passengers. Initially, passengers simply sat on sacks of mail or slats of wood, enduring freezing conditions over the mountains and scorching temperatures over deserts. In those first years, the sacks generally had a higher priority than the people, since the carriers were under contract to carry the mail and, ounce per ounce, cargo simply generated more revenue than passengers.

The fledgling airlines sold just 5,800 tickets in 1926 (in other words, barely an average of fifteen per day across the entire country), but by 1930, even with the Great Depression causing misery across the country, the number was up to 417,000. And while this was a literal fraction of the 708 million rail tickets sold that year, it was enough for the airlines to invest in much bigger planes, and to start putting as much focus on passengers as on mail. TWA, or Transcontinental & Western Air (Howard Hughes later simply changed the meaning of the initials to Trans World Airlines), introduced service that indeed crossed the continent, though it took twenty-seven hours with as many as fourteen refueling stops along the way.

It was against this backdrop that Ellen Church and Steve Stimpson cooked up the idea of stewardesses for Boeing Air Transport, which we know today as United Air Lines. And certainly the airline—indeed, any airline—was in need of savvy marketing angles to persuade the general public to fly. One less than brilliant promotion was a "wives fly free" offer in 1929 by Colonial Air Transport, a New England firm. The airline made the mistake of sending thank-you letters to the men's homes expressing gratitude to Mr. and Mrs. Smith for their business and hopes that it would see them again soon on another Colonial flight. It received numerous reply letters from angry wives saying they had never been on an airplane in their lives.

In truth, there was not much to recommend the endeavor. Airplanes were deafeningly loud, and often given to terrible vibrations when they hit pockets of turbulence that slammed against the cabin, especially when the craft was straining to get up over a mountain range like the Sierras or the Rockies.

The wicker chairs in early passenger planes didn't always stay bolted to the floor, so some passengers wound up with severe bumps, cuts, bruises, and even broken bones. But that was not the worst of the problems. The worst was the smell. "The airplanes smell of hot oil and simmering aluminum, disinfectant, feces, leather and puke," one pilot, Ernest K. Gann, said of commercial flight in the early 1930s.

Passengers were given ample supplies of reinforced paper bags politely known as "burp cups," and they were sorely needed. TWA research found that 80 percent of its passengers over the Southwest became airsick, and "airline officials even joked that they pasted pictures of the Grand Canyon on the bottom of air sickness containers so that everyone could see the Grand Canyon," noted Daniel L. Rust in his book *Flying Across America: The Airline Passenger Experience*. But the vibration and jolting were so bad that many still missed the target, or found that the bag wasn't strong enough to hold their volley without breaking apart in a soggy, putrid mess. (It would not be until 1949 that a man named Gilmore T. Schjeldahl invented a plastic-lined airsickness bag for Northwest Airlines, a pioneering feat that, along with his other patent breakthroughs in packaging, satellite balloons, and coronary catheters, secured him a place in the North Dakota Entrepreneur Hall of Fame.)

Another strategy was to open a window, because the airplanes flew low enough that pressurization was not a big problem, but this approach to throwing up had its own hazards. "If you stuck your head out to do this, you might find someone a few seats ahead with the same idea, and you could receive his blast in your own face," said aviation historian T. A. Heppenheimer.

In many passenger planes of the era, there were small vents near the base of the seats. These allowed the cabin to be quickly hosed down after a particularly severe flight but for those aboard, air travel was too often a pursuit that left people "reeking of vomit," as Gann, the pilot, described it.

Given this well-documented phenomenon as well as periodic airliner disasters that made for sensational news, such as the 1931 TWA crash that killed Notre Dame football coach Knute Rockne, it is a wonder that anyone flew at all. Yet the truth was that airplanes were getting stronger and more stable all the time, and with the introduction in 1933 of the ten-passenger Boeing 247 and a year later the fourteen-passenger Douglas DC-2, with metal construction and sealed air-controlled cabins, air travel was becoming vastly more comfortable, more pleasant, more kind to the stomach—and more safe. And, to strengthen its main appeal to begin with, it was becoming ever speedier: the 247 cut cross-country flying times to twenty hours, with six immediate stops.

"The transports of yesterday averaging 100 mph are now

obsolete," marveled the *New York Herald Tribune.* "What, eight hours to Chicago?! The new liners make it in 4¾ hours so that one may leave Newark Airport after the theater and a leisurely midnight repast and be in Chicago for breakfast." Or in San Francisco by the evening! "The Pacific by bed time," the article said, "sounds so much more economical of life's fleeting moments."

Given that they had a better product, the airlines needed a better way to sell it. And if the problem for the industry was to persuade a wary public to fly, what better ambassador could there possibly be than a young nurse with a ready smile? More subtly, since the great majority of travelers at that point were male businessmen, there was an inherent challenge to machismo involved in putting a stewardess on the plane. If this girl had the moxie to get on the plane, what guy worth his salt would chicken out?

Stimpson's bosses in Seattle weren't so sure. For all the comfort and cheer that young women might bring to the air, Boeing's initial reluctance was understandable. Just as there were stewards aboard ocean liners and porters on the railroads, the operative assumption had been that cabin staff on airplanes would be exclusively male. In fact, before Church got him so enthused about the idea of stewardesses, Stimpson, the traffic boss in San Francisco, had come up with a plan to hire young Filipino males to attend to Boeing's growing passenger load.

Now, though, Stimpson had seen the future, and she was walking on air. He was nothing if not relentless, and he took his idea over his boss's head and straight to the airline's president. Within a few weeks, he got the go-ahead, but with strict conditions. It would be a three-month trial, and any Boeing stewardess would indeed have to be a registered nurse, wearing a tunic-type uniform. He hired Church as the world's first airline stewardess, and he and she quickly drew up a manual, titled *Dos and Don'ts*, for all stewardesses to follow.

"A rigid military salute will be rendered the captain and co-pilot as they go aboard and deplane before the passengers," the manual said. "Check with the pilots regarding their personal luggage and place it onboard promptly." This was an ironic twist, given that no less a storied aviator than Lindbergh himself thought the cockpit might be a model for workplace equity between the sexes. "Women are just as well-fitted to operate a plane as men," Lindbergh told one reporter, "and the physical difference between them that may handicap women in other lines of work need not do so when it comes to flying."

The stewardess—it was intended as a temporary job title, Church said, until a "more suitable name" could be thought up—must address each passenger by name, and offer customers coffee, tea, or bouillon from jugs loaded onto each flight. She must be strong enough to help the pilot pull an airplane out of a hangar or push it into one. In the deep pocket of her apron she must carry three vital items: a wrench, a screwdriver, and a railroad timetable. (Airplanes generally navigated simply by following the route of the transcontinental railroads, and were often forced down by bad weather, so it would become the stewardess's job to redirect passengers to rail terminals if needed.) And on May 15, 1930, Boeing Air Transport introduced the "sky girls" on its ten-passenger Boeing 80 planes and its "mainline" route, which went from Oakland to Chicago by way of Cheyenne.

In the annals of marketing brainstorms, the idea of the stewardess ranks in the pantheon. Within a matter of weeks, Boeing found that it had hundreds of approving letters from passengers (nearly all of them male, though of course the vast majority of passengers were male), urging the airline to make the experiment permanent. Hollywood was fascinated, as were the popular magazines of the day, which had no problem picking up on the "psychological punch" Stimpson had envisioned in the letter to his superiors.

"The passengers relax," noted a reporter for *Atlantic Monthly* aboard a bumpy flight. "If a mere girl isn't worried, why should they be?"

Everybody seemed to love the concept—everybody, that is, except the wives of Boeing pilots, who organized their own fervent letter-writing campaign to the Boeing head office in a last-ditch, unsuccessful effort to stop the stewardesses from becoming permanent employees. It was no use, of course: Boeing Air Transport had a bonanza on its hands. It quickly hired twenty more women, all of them nurses, and by 1933 it had more than fifty. Its competitors—American, Eastern, Western, and Transcontinental & Western (later known as Trans World)—quickly followed suit.

The job of the stewardess was nothing less than to domesticate a hurtling metal tube in the sky. As an Eastern Air Lines manual for stewardesses in the mid-1930s put it, the air hostess's duties were "of a social nature, to set up a bridge party if a bridge game is desired, to serve coffee or a cup of tea and some tasty biscuits." If any female passenger had a crying baby, the stewardess was told to offer to take the baby and walk up and down the aisle, soothing the child. (Even if by some miracle one of today's harried flight attendants found that she, or he, had enough time to do that, it is hard to imagine airline lawyers signing off on the practice from an insurance standpoint.)

Strangely, though flying was statistically a far less safe proposition than it is today, and the hidden appeal of nurses was their ability to deal calmly with medical emergencies, there were no safety demonstrations by the attendants back then. Airlines didn't want to alarm passengers by even acknowledging the possibility of a crash; besides, there were no drop-down oxygen devices, and seats did not have removable cushions that could be used as flotation devices.

With planes carrying a maximum of twenty-one passengers and often less than full, stewardesses were encouraged to learn each passenger's name and to chat with them, even taking an empty seat alongside one of them for a more extended conversation or a game of cards. With fares tightly regulated by the government and nearly every carrier flying the DC-3, there were no price wars among the airlines and no big amenities like today's free satellite television or "an extra inch of pitch at your seat!" to differentiate them. So the big way for your airline to stand out was to have the best, friendliest, and most competent stewardesses.

The price of air travel, for most people, remained prohibitive—$260 round-trip across the country, or about $4,300 in today's money. But time is money, and many businesses deemed it worth the steep fares to be able to move their men—they nearly all were men at this time—around the country on a "three-mile-a-minute" airplane, as one United ad promised. For the airlines battling for this customer, there was simply no better ambassador to the air than an attractive young stewardess.

With America in a Depression, the mobility and presumed excitement of the stewardess's life quickly made her an icon. A 1933 article in the Toledo, Ohio, *Sunday Times* reported that the stewardess "has become the envy of stenographers in New York and [farmers'] daughters in Iowa. She seems to be on the way to becoming to American girlhood what policemen, pilots and cowboys are to American boyhood."

Boeing-United stewardess Olette Hasle explained to *Collier's* magazine in 1932 that the job involved being "a saleswoman, an information bureau, a diplomat, an entertainment committee, a dietitian." Another poked a little fun at her older, male passengers: "Usually I can read in your face before take-off whether you have flown before," she said. "If you're mature and filled with responsibilities your expression proclaims that you know you are to be killed and you've made up your mind to die bravely."

In 1940, United began distributing an in-flight magazine to passengers, and the very first edition was effusive about stewardesses in general and United's in particular. "If you select one group of American girls, which, more than any other, represent beauty as a class, it wouldn't be dancers, debutantes, chorus girls or the much glorified movie starlets," the magazine asserted. "It would not be models, they are more often pretty and vapid than beautiful. The one group today building up the right to that designation is the airline stewardess. They've got an alert look about them that's fascinating . . . and they can't have that world-weary expression which some girls believe devastating and everybody else regards as a pain in the neck."

By the end of the decade, with the airlines flying larger planes and launching new routes, nearly a thousand stewardesses were in the air. Quickly, some industry standards evolved. The stewardess should be no taller than five feet, four inches and weigh no more than 115 pounds. (Over time, as the planes grew larger, these limits were expanded to five feet, eight inches and 130 pounds.)

And before long, the Stimpsonian ideal—that a stewardess not be the "pretty type"—was amended, if not turned on its head. Attractiveness was very much in demand, not just in the face but all the way to the foot. "With all passengers seated in the plane, a hostess' feet are especially conspicuous," TWA explained in a 1935 information packet for applicants. "If you know that your feet are larger than average for your height and weight, we ask that you discuss the matter with the local TWA representative and possibly avoid an unnecessary trip"—to the job interview.

The work was hard and hazardous (at least eleven stewardesses were killed within the first five years), but it was also fun and, to a degree all but unimaginable today, stewardesses found themselves to be objects of an almost religious veneration. United stewardess Inez Keller, one of "The Original Eight," recalled that when her plane ran out of gas once and landed at a farm near Cherokee, Wyoming, the people in the area "came in wagons and on horseback to see the plane. They'd never seen an aircraft before and they wanted to touch it and to touch me. One of them called me 'the angel from the sky.'"

For the most part, the public was fascinated by airliners and by both the handsome heroes who commanded them and the vestal virgins who domesticated them. Airports became a curious form of free entertainment, perhaps especially sought out because Depression-era conditions, for many, made the idea of possessing an airline ticket as remote a possibility as a trip to Oz. In 1930, Dallas's Love Field and Kansas City Airport reported up to 25,000 and 30,000 visitors, respectively, on some summer weekends, even though neither airport had more than six departures and arrivals or a combined total of more than one hundred seats into or out of town on any given day.

"Image was so important back then, and the job was so exciting," recalled Helen McLaughlin, a stewardess in the 1940s for Continental and United. "Parents used to take their families on Sunday drives to the airport, and they would wait to see the hostess come out of the plane. We were always told to wave." F. Scott Fitzgerald offered a somewhat different take, from the passenger's point of view, in *The Last Tycoon*: "The younger people look at the planes, the older ones look at the passengers with a watchful incredulity. In the big transcontinental planes we were the coastal rich, who casually alighted from our cloud in mid-America." (In the Jet Age, such stops were no longer needed, of course, and so the great landmass between the coasts came to be called "flyover country.")

In Salt Lake City, a young woman named Margaret Macphail described going out to the airport one day with a male companion, joining a large, picnicking crowd to watch airplanes come and go. "Each word of conversation among us landlubbers," Macphail reported, "had contained both 'I wish' and 'I wonder.'" She and her male friend stayed until late in the evening, gazing at a darkening western horizon, looking for the lights of a plane.

The stewardesses were "masterly performers of womanhood," as historian Kathleen M. Barry puts it in *Femininity in Flight: A History of Flight Attendants*. "Stewardesses had to work quite hard to seem not to be working at all."

In a way, the pilot's job sounds far simpler. The guy had to fly the plane. A stewardess had to serve but seem happy to do it, be friendly but not too friendly, turn herself out immaculately, be alluring to the traveling businessman but not come off as inappropriate to the young mother next to him, flying with her baby to visit Grandma in Cleveland.

Shockingly enough, these beautiful, skilled, poised, friendly, and ambitious young stewardesses tended to meet and fall in love with eligible young men. That was fine by the airlines except for one thing: that meant the end of your stewardess job. Marriage (for stewardesses, not pilots) was a taboo, as was being pregnant, and for many airlines that remained the case for decades to come, changing only after years of legal challenges by the flight-attendant unions. United, for instance, did not lift that ban until November 7, 1968.

Stimpson, in a 1955 speech celebrating the twenty-fifth anniversary of stewardesses, said he knew of only one case in which the airline had looked the other way when a stewardess informed United that she was, in fact, married. "That was very early and we were in a great hurry," Stimpson recalled. "Miss Crawford [her full name then was Ellis Crawford Podola] would be out on a trip and be delayed by bad weather and/or other causes, sometimes for several days, and her husband would phone me around three o'clock in the morning and say, 'Mister, where is my wife?'"

One should perhaps not be too hard on the airlines for this policy, at least in the early decades. It was very much a cultural standard in the workplace that a woman's place, once she started having children, was at home. In most jobs, announcing that you were expecting was tantamount to handing in your resignation letter. Once kids came along, if not before, the man was expected to work at an outside job and provide, while the woman worked at home, looking after the family. While this was a societal ideal, it was also generally achievable as an economic matter; for most men, their salaries were enough for the entire family.

In any event, for a stewardess who loved her job but also loved a man, she had to choose one or the other. Many airlines, even the defunct ones, have huge alumnae associations of ex-stewardesses, which go by a name that is highly bittersweet: Clipped Wings. As sought-after as the jobs were, the turnover among most airlines was very high, averaging between a year and eighteen months. But that was just fine with the airlines: for every twenty-one-year-old "veteran" who left to get married, there were legions of fresh-faced nineteen-year-olds dreaming of winning a stewardess job.

The stewardess remained a powerful marketing draw for the airlines, and slowly but inexorably, the image of the ideal stewardess was undergoing a transformation. Somewhere along the line, she stopped being a plainly nurse. As an Eastern Air Lines ad in the 1960s put it, she needed to have "poise, intelligence, and good looks." That's why, the ad said, "We look at her face, her make-up, her complexion, her figure, her weight, her legs, her grooming, her nails and her hair." She became a trolley dolly, an outright sex object, perhaps most infamously, in the "Fly me" commercials of now defunct National Airlines in the early 1970s: "I'm Cheryl. Fly me"; "I'm Pat. I'm going to fly you like you've never been flown before"; and "I'm Laura. You can fly me any day of the week."

Dallas-based Braniff International even promoted "The Air-Strip," a brightly colored, Emilio Pucci–designed stewardess uniform with various components, which the young women were told to change around during the flight.

Beginning in 1953 and lasting all the way through January 1970, United Air Lines even had male-passengers-only flights every weekday between New York and Chicago called the Executive. Stewardesses lit the men's cigars and pipes (not allowed on other flights, though cigarettes were), and served them martinis and steaks. They brought slips of paper with the closing stock prices, relayed by the pilots via air traffic control, and the service was so popular that four years after it started, United added a second pair of flights each day.

In 1958, Edythe Rein, senior vice president of a New York firm that sold television rights, appealed to the Civil Aeronautics Board to open the flights to her gender. She lost her case. While the C.A.B. said it did not approve of "undue, unjust or unreasonable discrimination," it did not find the men-only flights amounted to that: after all, there were plenty of other flights that Rein could take to get to Chicago. Facing pickets from the National Organization for Women, and with changing cultural mores dropping demand for the flights to under 50 percent of capacity, United finally decided to drop them. On the last flight out of the Executive, a forty-nine-year-old businessman wistfully told a reporter: "You want to know the real reason we're here? It's not because of no women. It's because there are no squalling kids. We get enough of that at home."

Today, with most modern airliners packed full and the demand for low fares spurring elimination of "frills" such as food and personal attention, with a passenger–flight attendant ratio of fifty to one and with terrorism as a lurking concern, a passenger could be forgiven for thinking the airlines have reached a sort of "Fly Me? Go Fly Yourself" era.

But between the era of soothing nurses and the present one of crowd control in the air, stewardesses were the very height of chic and glamour. And in ways that today's harried travelers and overworked airline employees may find difficult to conjure, this ideal was used very consciously and quite brilliantly to sell an extremely alluring product around the world.

Again, as in the early days of passenger service, the jet-setting stewardess had to strike the perfect balance. She is "a beautiful person," as one Braniff International brochure put it. "She is alive for her interest in people themselves. She is a daughter to the middle aged; security to the confused; a heroine to little girls; a source of pride and joy to her parents." Next to a photograph of passengers relaxing in an airborne lounge, some sipping martinis, others enjoying coffee in silver service, Braniff said this of an air hostess: "She knows how to serve meals and beverages in a gracious manner, a little about aerodynamics, a lot about first aid, and even how to deliver a baby—just in case."

More literally, the product *was* the world. For if it took a generation to get from the Wright brothers to the bumpy, noisy, slow airplanes Stimpson was so intent on sprucing up with lively young nurses, it took only another generation to get to an era of almost limitless possibilities in the sky. It was now possible to go "Up, Up and Away" with TWA, or to "Fly the Friendly Skies" of United. American had "Something Special in the Air" and Eastern was the "Wings of Man." But that was when flying had reached a golden age of sorts, when the Jet Age was at its peak. For all the promise to come in this new era, however, and for all the accolades the British had received in the very first year of their pioneering efforts to enter the Jet Age, the second year of the magnificent Comet was a disaster—three of them, in fact.

six

The Comet Mystery

"Yoke Peter," the first Comet in service
(1952, top), and as reconstructed for
crash investigation (1954).

"I have made an examination of the hearts of a very great number of people who have died in the most extraordinary circumstances," reported Antonio Fornari, the director of the Institute of Forensic Medicine at the University of Pisa. "But I have never come across anything like this before."

This had been Professor Fornari's succinct account of the thirty-five deaths on board the de Havilland Comet that had exploded off Elba, in January 1954. And it posed the essential mystery before the man who was now charged by Prime Minister Churchill with finding out what was wrong with the airplane: Arnold Hall, the thirty-nine-year-old wunderkind of the British aviation industry.

Hall, a tall, rangy man with piercing blue eyes, was the director of the Royal Aircraft Establishment, the nerve center of the country's civilian airline program. In ordinary circumstances, this job was the best of challenges for an aeronautics professor such as Hall. He got to pick out the most promising aircraft, the brightest talent. The RAE, Hall once said, was "like a huge bottle of fizzing mineral water whose bubbles are ideas. My job is to decide which bubbles to capture, develop and arrange to be incorporated into future plans."

But with the third jet Comet having simply blown apart in the sky in less than a year, this one in April 1954 over the Bay of Naples, Hall summoned his top staff to the office at Farnborough and told them of Churchill's brief to him.

"I've called you in because we've been given the green light on the Comet investigation," said Hall, puffing on his ubiquitous pipe. "It has absolute priority over everything else we are doing and we've got to get on with it at top speed."

Hall was a congenitally curious man. Born in 1915, the son of a furniture dealer in Liverpool, he had spent most of his life experimenting with things. Once he nearly blew up his house, putting fireworks into the oven, to "see what would happen." He designed his own steam engine when he was a boy, and he was a star student at Cambridge, working under Melvill "Bones" Jones, a legendary professor. After the war, he had quickly gained coveted positions, as a professor of aeronautics at the University of London and head of the department of aeronautics at the Imperial College of Science and Technology in Kensington.

Now he was the chief detective on one of the biggest disaster investigations in history. The Comet victims had been killed in a split second, because of "violent movement and explosive decompression," according to the Italian professor, seconded by a London pathologist. Each had been ejected suddenly from their seat, either into the seatbacks just in front of them or against the sides and ceiling of the cabin. But what had caused the accident?

The elegant, triple-tailed Lockheed Constellation, the last great propliner before the jet era.
The Peter M. Bowers Collection at The Museum of Flight

William E. Boeing, founder of the Boeing Company.
The Museum of Flight

Rollout of the "Dash-80," the prototype for the Boeing 707. *The Boeing Company Collection at The Museum of Flight*

Bill Boeing (top)
shows Bill Allen
the Dash-80 under
construction (center).
Bill Allen holds the
roses as Mrs. Boeing
christens the jet
plane (bottom).
*The Boeing Company
Collection at The
Museum of Flight*

(In each photo) Bill Allen, Boeing's president, and Tex Johnston, the company's chief test pilot, along with another test pilot. *The Boeing Company Collection at The Museum of Flight*

The only photograph taken from the Dash-80 during Tex Johnston's famous "barrel roll." The plane is upside down. *The Boeing Company Collection at The Museum of Flight*

The Boeing 707
under construction.
*The Boeing Company
Collection at The
Museum of Flight*

Canada's Avro
Jetliner, the second
jet airliner to fly,
after the Comet.
*The Peter M. Bowers
Collection at The
Museum of Flight*

The British
Columbia
Centennial Air
Show, Canada,
June 1958.
*The Museum
of Flight*

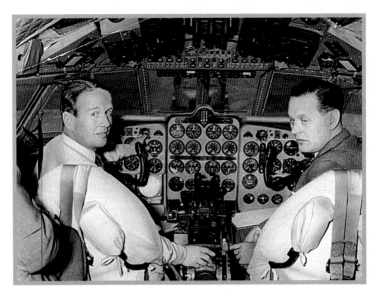

John Cunningham (left) in the cockpit of a Comet. Manchester Daily Express / *SSPL*

Tex Johnston, right, hands the 707 manual to Captain Scott Flower of Pan Am.
The Boeing Company Collection at The Museum of Flight

Solving the Comet mystery: the tank test at Farnborough, England, 1954.
Science Museum / SSPL

MENU

B.O.A.C. COMET 4
First-ever Transatlantic Jetliner

INAUGURAL FLIGHT

OCTOBER 1958

★

BRITISH OVERSEAS AIRWAYS CORPORATION

The Comet returns: the new Comet 4 begins transatlantic service in October 1958. *British Airways Heritage Centre*

An early ad for the new Jet Age. *Delta Air Transport Heritage Museum*

CLUB COMPARTMENT OF DELTA'S CONVAIR 880 JET

Delta's luxurious Jets follow the Sun – for fun!

For winterbound Northerners, a 15 degree change in latitude can bring a welcome 50 degree change in temperature and Delta Jets make the transition at 600 mph dozens of times each day ...for thousands across the nation to Florida and the Caribbean. No faster way than Delta's DC-8 and 880 Jets...nor any equal in personal attention or gracious hospitality — be it Delta Deluxe or economical Jetourist.

Delta routes serve Florida, Puerto Rico, Jamaica and Venezuela.

DELTA
the air line with the BIG JETS

The old—the Boeing 377 Stratocruiser (top)—and the new—the Boeing 707 Jet Stratoliner—1958. *The Boeing Company Collection at The Museum of Flight*

The explosion of a bomb? The collapse of the airframe? Disintegration of an engine? A catastrophic failure by the pilots?

"Every possibility must be examined," Hall told his staff. "We'll believe nothing until we've proved it, scientifically and conclusively. . . . We'll take every conceivable cause of aircraft failure and keep at it until we can honestly say it's been eliminated."

All the remaining Comet 1s were grounded, and would most certainly never carry passengers again—and one or more of them would be completely taken apart in Hall's investigation. There was an odd confluence of tragedy and triumph for the British nation. Just a month after the speediest airliner in history was taken off BOAC's Empire service, a Briton broke an entirely different speed mark. On May 6, 1954, Roger Bannister, that young medical student with a singular goal, became the first human on record to run a mile in under four minutes. For a few months after its maiden flight in May 1952, there had seemed to be nothing but good news about the de Havilland Comet and what *The Manchester Guardian* had proudly called Britain's "faster, simpler, safer" plane. In addition to thrice-weekly jet flights between London and Johannesburg, BOAC had carried out a weekly service to Ceylon (Sri Lanka), with more routes on the drawing boards—Tokyo, Hong Kong, Australia. "To halve the travel time across the world," proclaimed the airline's year-end management report, "is the most signal advance in international transport that we and our predecessors in title have been privileged to make in our history. B.O.A.C. has fathered the jet age in civil aviation, as in the past we pioneered the Empire routes and as in the future we intend to girdle the earth with all-British air service." The American press glumly took note as well: "The whoosh of British jets," said *The Wall Street Journal*, "is leaving U.S. passenger-plane competitors farther and farther behind."

True, the Comet seemed insatiable in its fuel use, having to stop every few hours for a reload, but it was the fastest thing going and passengers loved it. BOAC even claimed the booking rate was so high that the Comet was profitable—a claim that American aviators took with a grain of salt, given the subsidized nature of the Comet project. But now the American titans were interested, especially since de Havilland had a bigger Comet 2 in the works—it could carry as many as seventy-five passengers compared with the Comet 1's thirty-six, and its range would be 2,000 miles and possibly more, once the engineers were done, versus the smaller plane's 1,750 miles.

The most audacious request came from Rickenbacker of Eastern, who said that he wanted nearly three dozen of them and that the "Englishman" should start working overtime to produce them. ("Really now," one British aircraft builder was quoted as saying, "you cannot suddenly swell an industry to twice its size, you know.")

One drizzly evening in Rome, five and a half months after the inaugural passenger flight, the first of the de Havilland Comet's problems appeared. It was October 26, 1952. Just before seven o'clock, BOAC Captain R. E. H. Foote got his clearance from the tower controllers at Ciampino Airport, and a Comet with thirty-five passengers and eight crew members aboard roared down the runway. The plane was London-bound on the route from Johannesburg. As it gathered speed, Captain Foote later reported, the Comet, known as Yoke Zebra after the last two letters of its call name, began to pull slightly to the right, but he corrected the drift and, at 129 miles per hour, the plane left the runway and Foote said he called for "undercarriage up"—in other words, for the landing gear to be retracted, which cuts drag on the aircraft. Suddenly, however, he felt a strong pull to the left, and then, he said, the plane started to shudder—Yoke Zebra was going into a stall. Foote said he pushed forward on the control column, to control the plane's angle of landing, but it did not respond. The plane bounced hard, but fortunately landed on its tires, since there had been no time for the gear to retract.

The Comet skidded off the Italian runway and hit a muddy hill, ripping off part of the undercarriage and hurtling forward for another 270 yards before it came to a stop, ten yards from the airport's boundary fence. Parrafin fuel started pouring from the Comet's tanks, but miraculously, the airplane did not catch fire and everyone managed to scamper to safety. There were no major injuries.

Some airport attendants and BOAC staff on the ground praised Foote for his handling of the aircraft after what had initially looked like a normal takeoff. But that was not the official conclusion of BOAC, issued a few months later. It blamed the accident on "an error of judgment by the Captain in not appreciating the excessive nose-up attitude during take-off." Essentially, it said he had overcompensated for some minor drift in the plane. Captain Foote was demoted—taken off the Comet routes and placed on York propeller freighter aircraft. He was deeply embittered by the action, according to Derek N. Dempster, a British wartime pilot and aviation historian who interviewed Foote, believing he had done nothing wrong. Yet the order may have saved his life, given the Comet troubles to come.

On the night of March 2, 1953, a brand-new Comet, grandly named *Empress of Hawaii* and purchased by Canadian Pacific Airlines, made a scheduled stop at Karachi, Pakistan, en route to Sydney, where de Havilland had asked that it make a stop in order to carry out a sales pitch to Qantas, the Australian long-distance carrier. From there, it would fly a route to Hawaii and onward to Canada. Captain Charles Pentland, Canadian Pacific's director of overseas flight operations, was in command, and on board with him were ten other men, four from the airline and six from de Havilland's technical support team. They all freshened up and prepared to leave Pakistan shortly before dawn the next day.

Once again, a Comet roared down the runway and went nose up, but failed to gain altitude. This one slammed into a fence at the airfield and into a hill, exploding into a fiery ball. All the men perished, and a brand-new jet airplane became a burned metal heap.

A team of investigators, including the de Havilland chief test pilot, John Cunningham, flew to Pakistan and tried to unravel what had happened. Here the ultimate conclusion was somewhat mixed, for de Havilland and the British aviation establishment wound up sticking by the basic airworthiness of the plane—while recommending a modification of the leading edge of the wing that they said would give pilots a better "feel" for the aircraft.

In essence, the pilot of a Comet had to be very careful executing the nose-up maneuver that was part of the takeoff sequence. As the pilot manual put it, "Care should be taken not to overdo this and adopt an exaggerated tail-down attitude with consequent poor acceleration." The hydraulic system built into the jetliner was so effective that it was disturbingly easy to overdo it. The reshaping of the wing edge wound up giving a small extra margin of error, by improving the airflow and reducing the speed at which the entire airplane would go into a stall.

The modifications took only a few weeks, and soon the Comets were back in service. Not only did Britain's aviation leaders stubbornly stick by their airplane, they soon found themselves in a dispute with American regulators over how to determine safety standards for a *future* Comet that would be able to make the flight across the Atlantic Ocean to the United States. This was the very plane that Juan Trippe of Pan Am was speaking about with de Havilland, the Comet 3, and the U.S. Civilian Aeronautics Administration was raising numerous questions about design safety. These included the placement of the engines inside the wing, which some American regulators thought posed greater hazards in a fire than if they were on struts, and the level of noise and dark streaks of pollution made by the jet, a huge source of concern for people living near airports. Jets could actually be louder at lower speeds, because they were operating at less than maximum efficiency, not unlike the way a car with automatic transmission will make more noise in a lower gear.

More broadly, however, the American regulators were only beginning to think about the problem: after all, they had never had to certify a jetliner before, and this version of the Comet was a few years away from becoming a reality. But the British needed to have some sense of the rules now, since they hardly wanted to build a plane and then be told by a bunch of American aviation authorities that they would need to impose expensive modifications. The impasse infuriated Lord Brabazon, the chief British air advocate and the chairman of the UK Air Registration Board.

"A very curious and sinister situation has arisen recently," thundered Lord Brabazon. "Through the genius of our engine and airframe manufacturers and operators we have produced machines such as the Comet, ahead of all others in the world. . . . With astonishment we learned that America refuses to validate our certificates. They say they have no experience on which to base an assessment of our calculations.

"A plea of technical incompetence comes strangely from America," the Lord added. "We have not questioned their machines in the past although they were streets ahead."

The British were basically highly insulted, because they believed that if a machine was good enough for them, it should be good enough for the Americans. Moreover, some British leaders thought the U.S. regulators were doing the bidding of their domestic industry by delaying technical approvals for the long-range plane Pan Am said it wanted. It is, of course, unknowable just how severe this dispute might have become had the Comet not met with disaster elsewhere. But the Americans, it turns out, were asking good questions.

Despite the accidents at Rome and Karachi, the Comet 1 had flown 104.6 million passenger miles in its first year, carrying some 28,362 passengers in nearly 10,000 hours of flying time. And as horrible as the Karachi disaster had been, BOAC and the new Comet operators, including Air France, could point to a safety record of sorts: not a single paying passenger had perished aboard a de Havilland Comet.

But exactly one year to the day after the inaugural service from London, that changed, in a flash of explosions in an Indian monsoon just six and a half minutes after a BOAC Comet took off from Calcutta's Dum Dum International Airport. Aboard was a passel of dignitaries from Australia and India on their way to attend the coronation of the new Queen.

The Comet captain, Maurice Haddon, left late in the afternoon in the heavy rain, soon radioing that he was "climbing on track" for a northwesterly heading. The plane was passing through a very intense storm when it abruptly blew apart into three main pieces. A villager, Narayan Chandra Gosh, reported seeing a flash of bright light and then focusing his eyes to see at least part of an airplane on fire, falling across the darkening sky. After a few minutes, he said, when most of the wreckage was on the ground, he heard two more loud explosions, which presumably were fuel tanks being ruptured. In an eerie twist, the first pilot in the air to spot the wreckage on the ground was a man in charge of a York freighter—Captain Foote, the commander of the Comet that had stalled and crashed at Rome, half a year before. Forty-three passengers and crew were dead.

With the charred ruins of the Comet spread across several miles of the Indian countryside, both Indian and British investigators could see no obvious immediate reason for the total structural failure of the jet airplane. Both sabotage and a lightning strike were of course raised as theories, but an examination of the wreckage did not yield a definitive clue—no trace of explosives, no scorched line that would be expected with a strike.

Shri W. Srinivasan, an official with the Hindustan Aircraft Company and a member of the Indian investigation team, wrote in its report that there had been some sort of failure or pressure that "imposed a heavy down-load on the wings with the resulting failure at about rib number seven." There was some evidence that throttles had been moved back and forth, perhaps in an attempt to correct for the force of a gust that could have pushed up or down on the plane as it was trying to slice through the storm during its ascent to cruising altitude.

Whether this was the result of pilot error or failure in a critical part of the load, Srinivasan could not say, and the available wreckage was gathered up to be shipped to Great Britain for further analysis. But while stopping well short of any definitive conclusion of what had happened, Srinivasan did uncover one other vitally important point of evidence. It was one that de Havilland and BOAC ultimately downplayed, since they believed the aircraft had come apart at more than one location— that it was buffeted by a severe storm that tossed it so violently that it broke under that strain. Such storms were freakish, but they happened, and they had certainly brought down other big propeller planes in the past. On the other hand, a KLM pilot had passed through the same storm, and later recalled to investigators: "It was no worse than normal monsoon weather. I went straight through it."

Yet Srinivasan's detective instincts had homed in on a completely valid point of inquiry, and had they been followed up on more assiduously, it is certainly possible that the two Comet disasters to come—the two Italian accidents of 1954—could have been averted. However, to do so, the British aviation establishment would have had to conclude that the Comet had a flaw so severe that it would essentially have to be rebuilt entirely. This, it would not do.

The Indian report, issued five weeks after the accident, did conclude that the plane had been hit by an "unusually severe storm" and that the wreckage did not indicate any obvious sign of sabotage, material defect, or poor workmanship. It, too, pointed to the problem of a pilot not getting the proper "feel" of the control system, and suggested that de Havilland explore whether it could modify that system "in order to give the pilot a positive 'feel' of air loads exerted on the control surfaces."

But Srinivisan noted, in the appendix, that the wing of the aircraft had undergone a standard test in which an extremely heavy load—heavier than what would normally be encountered in flight—is put on the wing to calculate its breaking point. On one, smaller patch of the wing, both static and fatigue (bending) tests were performed, and the wing failed at about 90 percent of the so-called ultimate (or abnormal) load. De Havilland later said that this was not an unexpected result, since the particular piece of sheet metal had been folded back and forth like a paper clip and was obviously not likely to pass a subsequent test. The piece of metal involved was replaced and never used in flight, and the 90-percent figure was signed off on by the company's engineers, since that was considered so far above the safety margin.

Perhaps that was a valid explanation, but it clearly did not satisfy Srinivisan, since he was so careful to include this point in the report. "The fatigue failure during static test occurred at rib number seven where the construction changes from two heavy spars to an outboard shell construction," he noted. "In this accident, again the wings have significantly failed at rib seven."

The Indian crash was a tragedy, but neither the Indian nor British inquiry concluded that it was an avoidable one—and therefore the Comet kept flying. It had no major mishaps for the rest of 1953, other than an incident aboard one of the French airliners that came in heavy at an airstrip in Dakar, Senegal, in French West Africa, and landed past the end of the runway. There were no major injuries. Moreover, the Comet 2 had begun to fly, bigger and a bit faster, so the main news in the papers about the Comet was about how it was breaking speed records around the world. Certainly, there were plenty of people who had no desire to fly aboard the speeding jet, and plenty of questions about the Comet, from the Indian investigator's nagging doubt to the continuing efforts of the aggrieved Captain Foote to clear his name. But with the top officials at both BOAC and de Havilland insisting the Comet was a perfectly airworthy plane, there were also plenty of people clamoring to climb aboard it, to experience the future of air travel. Bookings were solid. The plane that *Time* had called the "queen of the airways" was set to make 1954 a banner year.

Within hours of the mysterious disintegration of Yoke Peter over the Italian sea, BOAC announced a halt to all Comet service, and a salvage operation was quickly put together to pull as much evidence as could possibly be gathered from the wreckage at sea. But neither the airline nor de Havilland was willing to suggest at that point that the jetliner was a flawed airplane. "As a measure of prudence," said Sir Miles, "the normal Comet passenger services are being temporarily suspended to enable minute and unhurried technical examination of every aircraft in the Comet fleet to be carried out at London Airport."

A few days later, BOAC issued a statement that the initial inspection of all seven Comets remaining in the fleet showed "no evidence of structural weakness," and it floated a possible explanation of the tragedy: "The possibility of sabotage cannot be overlooked."

British aviation authorities agreed. "Considering the medical evidence, the bomb theory is a possible interpretation of what might have occurred," said Alan Lennox-Boyd, the minister for transport and civil aviation, returning from Rome, where he had attended a church service for the Elba victims. Security investigators were sent to every airport along the route of the doomed jet to see if anything had seemed amiss, if any suspicious package might have been checked on board the airplane.

Newspapers in Britain and beyond reported widely on the

sabotage theory, and it certainly seemed a plausible explanation for how an airliner could suddenly blow apart in the sky. *Truth*, a Sydney newspaper, even put a dummy time bomb aboard a propeller airliner. "It Can Happen Here," the headline proclaimed.

No one really knew what had caused this most recent crash of the Comet. The wreckage was slowly being salvaged, and there was simply no evidence of a bomb. On the other hand, as time passed and with BOAC losing £50,000 a week with the remaining Comets out of service, the airline began to press for a return of jet service to the skies. The Comet's certificate of airworthiness had not been withdrawn and, in what the airline portrayed as an abundance of caution, a committee led by Charles Abell, a respected aviation engineer, proposed some extra safety measures. Chief among them was some extra armor plating around the engines, as one of many theories floating around about the Elba disaster was that a turbine blade might have flown loose, puncturing one of the fuel tanks and precipitating an explosion. One operations official for BOAC, Sir Victor Tait, put up a different theory; that metal somewhere along the fuselage might have become weakened, or torn, causing the pressurized air inside the cabin to split the plane open as it forced its way out. De Havilland engineers insisted that was not possible. The plane's fuselage was too strong, and had been inspected repeatedly during maintenance checks.

The Comet still had its many cheerleaders, including the mighty Lord Brabazon of Tara. "Although no definite reason for the accident has been established, modifications are being embodied to cover every possibility that imagination has suggested as a likely cause of the disaster," he wrote to the Transport Ministry. "When these modifications are completed and have been satisfactorily flight tested, the Board sees no reason why passenger services should not be resumed."

Sir Miles, the head of BOAC, remained a vigorous Comet proponent, and his word carried great sway—especially with the pilots. A powerfully built Welshman who could be at turns the most genial fellow in the world and the most brusque, Sir Miles had been swept into the chairman's role in 1949, after a long tenure at Morris Motors, with a mandate to shake up the BOAC culture. He did not disappoint those who wanted change, though he made enemies in mid-level management, whom he memorably described in 1950 as "mostly large, ebullient gentlemen" who were "first class golfers" and whose "deliberations usually ended in a kind of relaxed compromise in which a programme for action was invariably missing." Sir Miles fumed over "the cloying sense of lushness, that money did not matter." He slashed the work force from 24,000 to 17,000 and cut directors' annual pay in half, from £1,000 pounds to £500, but he did not touch the piloting staff. "They are the salt of the earth," said the chairman, himself a World War I–vintage pilot in Mesopotamia and Persia and the holder of a Distinguished Flying Cross, who never tired of swapping flying stories with the pilots.

So there was considerable pressure to put the Comets back in service, and there was a matter of national prestige and economics on the line. Moreover, the pilots were loyal to Sir Miles and shared his basic confidence in the airplane. De Havilland was

out actively selling the new versions of the Comet on the drawing board, and Great Britain still believed it could beat the
Americans or anyone else in a battle for supremacy in the Jet
Age. If so, for an economy still struggling to recover its place in
the world after being pushed to the brink by World War II, the
hard currency from world jetliner sales would be a huge shot in
the arm. The Comet, as one newsreel from the era put it, "is
Britain's airborne answer to the problem of the dollar gap."

None of this, in retrospect, can excuse a decision to put a
death trap back in the skies, but it does explain the context for
the decision. And there was another reason, which to our minds
today is perhaps difficult to comprehend. Simply put, flying was
more of a risky business back then. An accident in the air was a
tragedy, but these things happened. Many people could not afford to fly in the first place, others refused to fly altogether. For
those who did fly, there was a ubiquitous reminder of risk, all
but vanished from airports today but a staple in airports of the
1950s and 1960s: insurance. Sold at ticket booths, at kiosks, and
even in vending machines, and costing just a few dollars but
good only for the duration of the flight, these policies were a
stark reminder to the air traveler: There's no guarantee you'll
get out of this thing alive. So why not buy some extra protection
for the family if your plane goes down?

While the Comet disasters up to and including Elba raised
serious questions about the safety of the airplane, they were hardly
a problem unique to the new, futuristic jetliner. The big propeller-
driven American-built airplanes crashed mysteriously as well,
with more people dying because those planes were larger than the

first-generation Comets. The DC-6, for instance, crashed three times in 1952, with 107 deaths total, three times in 1953 with 123 killed, and three times in 1954, with sixty-three dead. The Convair CV-240 crashed three times in 1953—eighty-eight dead in all. Just four days after the Comet crash over Elba, a Philippines Airlines DC-6 had crashed and burned while heading in for a landing at Rome, killing all sixteen people on board.

And so, just ten weeks after the Elba disaster—with no finding yet on the cause, and with no clear explanation yet for the Calcutta tragedy, either, other than the idea that the Comet had been taken down there by a freak weather event—the de Havilland Comet was allowed back into service. It was an astonishing act of hubris, and yet the Comets were booked at or near capacity by a trusting public. Sir Miles himself flew on the jet to demonstrate his confidence in it.

"We obviously wouldn't be flying the Comet with passengers were we not wholly satisfied that the conditions are acceptable for carrying passengers anywhere in the world," Sir Miles told reporters at London Airport.

Just sixteen days later—unbelievably, inexplicably—disaster befell another Comet. Again, it was a plane that had just left the Rome airport. This one was headed for Egypt, and if there was one thing for certain in this tragedy, it was that the weather could not be blamed. It was a beautiful evening over the Mediterranean, so much so that a passenger had begun the letter to his sweetheart commenting on the loveliness of the light.

Shortly before seven, Captain Wilhelm Mostert of the Comet G-ALYY, known as Yoke Yoke after its last two call letters, checked in with air traffic control. "I am bound for Cairo, where my estimated time of arrival is 2120," reported Captain Mostert. "I am ascending to 35,500 feet."

Though the plane had the BOAC livery, it was technically a charter flight, operated for South African Airways, and all had not gone so smoothly. In fact, the South African crew reported a problem on the initial leg of the journey, from London to Rome. A fuel gauge was faulty, failing to indicate just how much fuel there was in one of the tanks. It was not a problem that lent itself to a quick fix at Rome, and eventually a part had to be flown in from England. By the time the Comet took off from Ciampino, it was a full day behind schedule.

At some point after the captain's transmission, the Comet simply disappeared from the radar screen. It was somewhere between Naples and Stromboli, but there was no immediate word of its fate. At three in the morning, the telephone rang at Sir Miles's bedside table, and a reporter from the *News Chronicle* said excitedly that he had spotted a communication from Hamburg that another Comet was in trouble, overdue, and missing. "I shook the sleep from my eyes," Sir Miles recalled, "and told him that there could not be any Comets flying anywhere near Hamburg and that he had better check before he printed anything."

But shortly thereafter, the telephone rang again, this time from the BOAC operations room. "This time the whole world collapsed around me," said Sir Miles. Another Comet had simply disintegrated, killing everyone aboard.

Search crews found bits of wreckage, including the mysterious letter, scattered over several miles of the Bay of Naples, and by dawn of the next day they began to find bodies. As with the Elba disaster, the coroner noted something curious about the faces of those who had perished. They were strangely peaceful. Death, it seemed, came without warning.

Sir Miles quickly called the transport minister and they agreed that all the jetliners would be grounded. Trying to comfort him as he felt the edge of emotional collapse, his wife, Hylda, made him some bacon sandwiches and tea. "From that day to this," Sir Miles wrote a decade later, "whenever I taste or even smell bacon on toast my memory flashes back to that horrible dawn when, for the second time, my aspirations and expectations had literally fallen out of the sky."

This disaster was the death knell for the entire first fleet of de Havilland Comets. The Comet 1 and 1A models would never carry passengers again, except those who volunteered to be part of Professor Hall's investigation. The plane's certificate of airworthiness was withdrawn by the British authorities, and Prime Minister Churchill announced the massive investigation into what was causing the jetliner to fall apart in the air. But the Comet was not exactly being abandoned: officially, the hope was that once the Comet mystery was solved, the Comet—redesigned if necessary—would fly again.

Perhaps in the United States, a jetliner as tragically doomed as the Comet would be renamed as part of its redesign. In Great Britain, there seems to have been no great sentiment for an identity change, and BOAC proudly, stubbornly, kept its order for the Comet 2s and 3s on the books, even as airlines elsewhere in the world, including Pan Am, canceled their orders after the two Italian disasters.

"Whatever doubts may exist about Comet I, there can be none about its successor," proclaimed Lord Beaverbrook's *Evening Standard*. "The aim must now be to speed production . . . to ensure that as many as possible of these magnificent aircraft will be in service as soon as possible."

No one was more determined to see the Comet reclaim its good name than Geoffrey de Havilland. Now seventy-one years old, the man who lost two of his three sons in accidents involving de Havilland aircraft could not fully accept that the first jet airliner in the world was doomed. "To many of us it was the shattering blow of sudden and complete failure following on notable achievement that was the hardest to bear," he would recall a decade later. "We felt that it must be possible to seek out and remedy the unknown failure in a short time.

"The idea of giving up on the Comet was never seriously contemplated," he added. "It had just got to be made right." De Havilland was severely remorseful over the disasters, and told his colleagues: "All my life I have just seen improvements that could be made in the machine of the moment and tried to make them."

For de Havilland, the Comet tragedies were, in fact, only compounded by the pain and guilt he felt over the deaths of his sons in de Havilland aircraft, and the subsequent breakdown and death of his first wife. While he occasionally rationalized to friends that at least the boys had died doing what they loved, he also said that their deaths would not be completely in vain if they helped to build the knowledge whereby flight safety could be ever improved. The Comet's terrible failure seemed to make a mockery of such hope.

Lord Selkirk and others tried to buck him up, in part by emphasizing that de Havilland would be heavily involved in the investigation, and the solution. And Selkirk tried, on a broader level, to revitalize a demoralized nation as well: "It should be recognized," he said, "that this is not a time for despair, but rather a challenge to the whole engineering and scientific ability of this country."

But as Arnold Hall's investigation unfolded, there was no immediately obvious problem and no quick fix—and it was decided, prudently, to halt all construction on the next-generation Comets until the flaw in the pioneer models could be detected. With sabotage or massive engine failure ruled out, there was still the question of how three Comets could simply break apart in the sky, and there was another lingering question. Was there a "Rome jinx," as some BOAC officials began to put it? What were the odds that two jetliners would explode shortly after takeoff from the same airport, within a matter of weeks of each other?

Working with Doctor Fornari's conclusions as well as reconstructions of small model Comets with dummies, Hall's team quickly realized that many of the broken or crushed limbs of the victims occurred after death. What killed them was the sudden, violent decompression of their lungs. This was consistent with an explosion, but there were no traces of a bomb, nor was there any indication of a fire in any of the engines. Something had simply ripped the Comet apart.

Clearly, more needed to be understood about how the forces of pressurization and depressurization might work on the airplane, and Hall hit upon an ingenious solution—one that could simulate those forces more rapidly than putting an actual airplane back and forth in the sky, and in fact avoid the risk of repeated flights altogether. Professor Hall decided to put the fuselage of a de Havilland Comet into a giant sealable water tank with the wings sticking out of the side—as one observer put it, it looked like a giant shoe box waiting to take off. And with hydraulic jacks flexing the wings to simulate flight loads, with a quarter-million tons of water filling the tank and then being partially drained out, the Comet known as Yoke Uncle went through the pressurization cycles—over and over, twenty-four hours a day, seven days a week.

As the tank work was going on, Hall's team was busy with other detective work as well. Pieces from the salvage operation kept arriving, so that ultimately the investigators were able to piece about two-thirds of it together on a giant scaffold—a remarkable accomplishment for both the naval salvage team and those working at Farnborough.

The tests on the flying dummies that Hall's team had made also yielded clues about explosive decompression, offering victims' families the small solace of knowledge that death had been virtually instantaneous. As Hall later put it in his appearance at the official Court of Inquiry: "Those sitting near the breach were thrown right out, and those at the tail end would be tangled up in the wreckage. It would be all over in a fraction of a second." The dummies revealed an odd British attention to detail: one was dressed in a blue worsted three-piece suit, a blue-striped shirt, blue socks, and a black pair of oxford shoes, size 8. Another had a brown-checked jacket, gray flannels, and a gray sleeveless jersey. A third wore a gray suit with a fawn-and-brown cardigan. As was the case in the actual disaster, many of the dummies had much of their clothing intact, despite being in a plane that blew apart and despite their descent thousands of feet to the sea.

The cabin of the Comet was designed to have a pressure equal to that one would experience at 8,000 feet—roughly speaking, Denver plus a half-mile of altitude gain—when it was flying at 40,000 feet. This sort of pressurization, which we of course take for granted in jet travel, was a relatively new feature of airliners, and it exerted considerable force on the airplane's fuselage as it rose from an unpressurized state at takeoff to a pressurized one during its ascent, and then went the other direction as the plane descended for a landing. De Havilland said that the fuselage, which was encased in a relatively thin sheet of alloy metals, was tested to withstand both far greater pressure and far many more flights than an aircraft would ever encounter in a lifetime of service. Yoke Uncle, the Comet whose registration was G-ALYU, had already been through 1,221 cabin pressurization cycles and 3,539 flying hours when it arrived at Farnborough. With each five-minute fill-and-flush water cycle the equivalent of a three-hour flight, Yoke Uncle would go through nearly another 2,000 such cycles, in effect aging the aircraft about thirty-eight times faster than if it had been flying in normal service. One morning in late June 1954, Yoke Uncle yielded an astonishing clue.

A tiny crack in one of the windows had ripped apart. In simple terms, it was metal fatigue. This microscopic fracture would go undetected but, at some point, abruptly rip apart. For those aboard the Comet, it was a form of roulette. For hundreds of flights, the plane would be fine; but suddenly on the next one, that tiny crack would grow. This would cause the fuselage to crack like a tear in a piece of fabric, or a bend in a paper clip that holds despite repeated flexing—then breaks in two.

"You may know nothing at all about it," said Sir Lionel Heald, the Crown representative at the Inquiry, "until a disastrous fracture suddenly occurs without warning."

The pieces of the mystery slowly began to fit together. One important indication of how explosive the accident was came when investigators discovered one day that tiny bits of fiber from the carpeting in the interior of the cabin had been blasted with such force that they were embedded into the tail of the airplane.

But it was the tank test on Yoke Uncle that offered the definitive proof.

De Havilland executives and British regulators insisted that they had engineered the Comet well past any such fracture point, and defended themselves repeatedly by saying the phenomenon of metal fatigue, as it applied to a jetliner going through compression and decompression cycles, was not fully understood until the Hall inquiry provided definitive new knowledge. Lord Brabazon even argued that the original decision to keep flying the Comet after its mysterious crashes was justified.

"The Comet was a machine that was being talked about all over the world, being as it was, the most remarkable machine in the world, and if we grounded the type of every aircraft that had unexplained accidents you would scarcely have a machine in the air," he told the Inquiry court.

"It is metallurgy, not aeronautics, that is in the dock," Lord Brabazon insisted.

But that is not quite true. Metallurgy is part of aeronautics, and the Comet calculations were simply wrong. The possibility of metal fatigue was certainly raised during the Comet's design and its certification—after all, de Havilland had maintained that the plane would withstand it in the course of a regular flight life of the aircraft. It is true that de Havilland had tested the plane and conformed with accepted knowledge about metal fatigue, but it is not true that no one had envisioned a scenario in which fatigue could strike an aging airliner. In fact, Nevil Shute, a British engineer and writer, had even written a novel, published in 1948, *No Highway*, whose plot featured an expert warning about precisely this phenomenon—metal fatigue. Shute is perhaps best known for his postapocalyptic novel *On the Beach*, published in 1957, in which fallout from a nuclear war is slowly enveloping the earth, killing all animal life. While that peril has haunted mankind since Hiroshima, it did not come to pass in Shute's lifetime. But *No Highway* was eerily prescient of a real-life disaster. Hollywood made it into a movie, *No Highway in the Sky*, starring Jimmy Stewart as the absentminded professor who warns of the problem while flying aboard an airliner called the Reindeer—surely a sly allusion to the Comet, since one of Santa's reindeer happens to share that name. The film came out in 1951—a year before the de Havilland Comets went into service, and two years before the disaster near Calcutta, the first of three incidents in which the airplane simply fell apart in the sky, because of the very problem that Shute had envisioned.

Moreover, the Ministry of Supply, in the process of certifying the plane, had initially questioned whether the Comet fuselage could be guaranteed against fatigue beyond a thousand hours of flight time—less than a year of expected service time for a jetliner. The full stress testing of the Comet would be completed in due course, according to a memorandum of understanding among de Havilland, BOAC, and the Royal Aircraft Establishment—but *after* the plane started flying in 1952. It was a puzzling point of contention, and the parties involved said the proper testing was ultimately carried out. No one was ever found criminally liable for any aspect of the Comet disasters—essentially, the Court of Inquiry found, they had operated on the best available information at the time. As Sir Arnold Hall put it: "They built the Comet around the most advanced engineering knowledge available and could certainly not be held to blame."

The explanation never satisfied everybody involved, of course, but it was widely accepted, as was the general determination to go ahead with a revised model of the jetliner. Not everyone, of course, was persuaded that the Comet could take back the crown. When Baron Ernst Walter Hives, the head of the British Rolls-Royce Aero Division, came to Seattle in 1955 to take a look at the Dash-80, he walked quietly around the jet airplane and said softly, "This is the end." "The end of what?" asked George Schairer, his host and a top Boeing engineer. "The end of British aviation," said Baron Hives. Still, with a stronger fuselage, oval windows, and reinforcement at every possible stress point, a redesigned Comet could certainly fly, the Comet inquiry ultimately concluded. And so, also in 1955, British Overseas Airways Corporation issued a statement. "It has been decided," BOAC said, "to instruct the de Havilland Company to proceed with building a fleet of New Comets. The Corporation is satisfied that the cause of failures of the Comet I has been found out and can be eliminated by strengthening the fuselage structure."

But the Comet had lost years and lives, and it was simply unclear whether the new model would have any appeal to airlines besides the national carrier of Great Britain. Meanwhile, Britain's aviation industry had suffered yet one more indignity. Even its new, larger Britannia, a propeller-driven airplane, would not be ready in time for the Queen's visit to America in 1957. She would have to fly in a Douglas DC-7 instead. "At a time when state visits carry more prestige and importance than ever before," sighed the London *Daily Sketch*, "we are obliged to give the world a humiliating instance of Britain's dependence on America."

seven

The Race to Shrink the World

I'll put a girdle round about the earth
In forty minutes.

—*Puck, in* A Midsummer Night's Dream

And so, a great race was on. It would take years for a winner to emerge, but the crown prize was now certainly achievable—passenger service across the Atlantic Ocean. The Jet Age, tragically aborted by the Comet disasters, could begin again, and this time in earnest and around the world.

In England, with the Comet's designers now having found and fixed the plane's catastrophic flaw, BOAC announced that it was fully committed to the de Havilland Comet 4—a plane that would be safer, bigger, and faster than its tragic progenitor. Boeing was about to put its prototype, the Dash-80, up in the air for inspection. Douglas Aircraft, the dominant commercial airplane manufacturer up to that point, was running months if not years behind the Seattle upstart, but now it was in the game. It would build a jetliner called the DC-8. It had no prototype to show anyone, but Douglas insisted that was an advantage: it was all ears. Sure, go look at Boeing's airplane, the company said, but then come talk to us and we'll build something better.

"In our business, the race is not always to the swiftest or the first to start," soothingly explained Donald Douglas, Sr., the company's founder. And he had this to say: "There may be some distinction in being the first to build a jet transport. It is our ambition at Douglas to build the best and most successful."

It sounded reasonable, and Douglas could certainly play up its unbroken string of winners in the airliner business and its long-standing relationships with major airlines such as American and United. Douglas salesmen acknowledged that Boeing was a perfectly good military airplane manufacturer, but they openly disrespected the Seattle company's losing streak on the civilian side. Boeing, they said, simply didn't know how to build a good airliner.

Howard Hughes entered the fray, and represented more vividly than anyone else the astounding conversion that airline executives had gone through in a few short years—from once thinking of every reason not to go to jetliners but now practically falling over each other to be first in the sky with them. Hughes, once confident that the elegant, prop-driven triple-tailed Constellation would remain the queen of the skies for years to come, was now obsessed with the notion that TWA must be *the* airline to introduce jet travel to the United States.

Hughes called officials at Convair, a smaller manufacturer recently absorbed by General Dynamics, a defense conglomerate. Convair officials were extremely leery of the eccentric millionaire. A few years earlier he had discussed building an airplane with them, in negotiations Hughes insisted be conducted by flashlight in the middle of the night at the Palm Springs municipal dump. The plans went nowhere. He was odd and getting odder. He liked to fly airplanes in his bare feet; he got a much better feel for them that way, he explained.

Still, no one doubted that Howard Hughes was a genius, and this time Hughes convinced the manufacturer that he was quite serious, and he told them to put a move on it. In an impressive show of speed and skill, Convair engineers came up with two options for long-range jets. One was a four-engine model quite similar to the 707. The other was for a much larger plane, with six engines and room for all kinds of perks, from spacious bars to double sleepers. Hughes became fascinated with the latter design, which proved to be a remarkably prescient variant of the "jumbo jets"—the DC-10, the Lockheed L-1011, and the Boeing 747—which came into fashion in the 1970s.

But Hughes could not commit, one way or the other. He put off a decision and became distracted by a plan of his to return to his glory days as a Hollywood moviemaker. He commissioned an aide to travel to Atlantic City with the idea of signing no less than ten Miss America contestants to movie contracts. TWA's president, Ralph Damon, warned in a memo in December 1955 that unless the airline moved rapidly toward a decision, it would wind up in "splendid isolation" in the industry, "outclassed in speed, comfort, passenger acceptability, and economics." Hughes was as torn as Hamlet. He was tempted to go with the big plane; but no, he said, maybe better to do what his competitors were doing. A month after he sent his memo, Damon, "bitter and frustrated, died of a heart attack," wrote Donald L. Barlett and James B. Steele in their biography *Empire: The Life, Legend, and Madness of Howard Hughes*.

The race for a jet empire in the sky was not limited to the United Kingdom and the United States. In fact, in an all but forgotten twist to the competition, Canada had entered the arena a full half-decade before the Americans, putting a prototype medium-range jetliner up in the air in 1949, less than two weeks after the de Havilland Comet had made its first test flight. The four-engine Canadian Avro C102 Jetliner was sleek and handsome, and in many ways was a highly prescient precursor to the small jetliners, such as the Boeing 737 and DC-9, that became ubiquitous in subsequent decades for short-haul low-fare flights, especially in the United States and Europe. Yet again, Howard Hughes had been involved in this saga: he liked the plane and recognized, perhaps better than anyone else, its potential—it could be used to great effect in the Boston–New York and New York–Washington shuttles, and could get northeastern travelers to vacation spots in the South in half the time of the current planes going. He discussed a contract with the Canadian firm, but finally decided the fuel demand was too great. It was simply too early to make a commitment. Trans-Canada Air Lines, now known as Air Canada, also balked.

Unlike the British, the Canadians hardly saw a national jetliner as a prestige project—in fact, many in Parliament saw it as utter folly. The government ordered a halt to the Avro Jetliner program in 1951, and the sole prototype Jetliner was eventually cut for scrap, with only the nose and cockpit left to put in the Canadian Aviation Museum in Ottawa. It is a pity that the full aircraft did not survive for display, and it is difficult not to consider the Avro a giant missed opportunity for Canadian industry, since the fuselage was so close to what the market wound up wanting and improvements in jet technology would rapidly cut down on the fuel use that so concerned Hughes. In any event, while the Comet will forever keep its crown as the first jetliner to fly and the first to provide commercial service, the Avro takes second place in the former category and a what-if asterisk in the latter.

Two other national jetliner projects bear mention. With the Comet out of commission and the American jetliners not due out for passenger service until 1958, the Soviet Union wound up claiming a two-year period in which it could boast of having the world's only jet service—and, arguably, the first sustained such service since the Comet's run proved so erratic. Beginning in September 1956, Aeroflot, the giant state-run airline, flew twin-engine, fifty-passenger Tupolev Tu-104 jets between Moscow and the Siberian city of Irkutsk, with a stopover in Omsk. This cut the flying time between the two cities at either end of the route from nearly fourteen hours to seven hours, forty minutes, and the technological achievement was a source of great satisfaction to Premier Khrushchev, who surprised Western leaders by flying into London Airport on a 1956 state visit aboard his own

Tupolev jet. Some British reporters let on their envy—or perhaps it was mockery of the proletariat leader, or a touch of both—with descriptions of the plane's sumptuous "Victorian" interior of mahogany, copper, leather, and lace. The Tu 104 was widely believed to be a monstrously expensive project, though the true numbers were not revealed by Soviet leaders, and under Cold War restrictions it was never sold to or put in service by airlines outside the Soviet bloc.

Picking up where Canada left off, a French company that became known as Sud Aviation jumped into the game in 1955 with an elegant medium-range aircraft called the Caravelle. The jetliner's twin engines were mounted on the back of the airplane, giving a sleek, clean line to the wings. The plane was perfect for short intra-Europe flights—it started passenger service in 1959 on Air France's routes from Paris to Rome, Athens, Istanbul, and London. It proved itself such a contender in that market that United Air Lines wound up ordering twenty of them as well, for shorter hops on its domestic routes.

The Caravelles did not have a long enough range to fly across the Atlantic Ocean, however, so the race to be first on that route came down, in the end, to two contenders. On the British side of the ring, it was once again BOAC, Geoffrey de Havilland's company and a plane called the Comet 4. On the American side, there was Juan Trippe's Pan Am, Bill Allen's Boeing, and a sparkling new airplane, originally called the 707 Jet Stratoliner. In perhaps a nod to the very sleekness of the Jet Age, people soon stopped calling the airplane by such a cumbersome name, however. So the Boeing plane was destined to be known simply by its numerals, not quite an anagram of the numeral assigned to Agent James Bond, but an iconic arrangement of digits nonetheless. This plane, the first American jetliner, would forever be known as the Seven Oh Seven.

Boeing had moved aggressively into a sales campaign. "Here's the skyliner that'll bring the Jet Age to you," proclaimed one ad for the 707. "When you travel by Boeing jet," another promised, "two weeks is time enough for a vacation anywhere!" (Memo to bosses, circa 2010: Sounds good to me.)

Then there was Frank Slattery, sound asleep in his seat on a Boeing 707. "Here's Frank Slattery, taking his wife and children on vacation," read the headline underneath a photo of the dozing, bespectacled Frank, in a magazine ad. "He's not bothered by other drivers, detours, back seat squabbles or too many stops." On a Boeing jetliner, the ad explained, "he's above all that."

In perhaps the most famous company advertisement, which ran in *Look*, *Life*, and other popular magazines of the mid-1950s, the wonders of jet travel were summarized with this headline: "The coin, the watch and the flower."

The ad depicted a woman in a neat blue dress with a pearl necklace and matching earrings as well as a fresh corsage, sitting happily next to a boy in a black-and-white suit and bow tie, holding a wristwatch to his ear. A Franklin dollar was balanced on its edge, so smooth was the flight. Plus, the ad promised, the

707 cabin "will be so quiet you will be able to hear the ticking of a watch. The flower you bought when you left will be fresh when you arrive."

That was in public. Privately, the company took yet another audacious step, inviting airline executives out to Seattle to see a confidential company production—a short film with the jarring title of *Operation Guillotine.* Boeing's in-house archivist, Mike Lombardi, tracked down the old reel-to-reel film for me, blew some dust off a projector, and together we watched what happened when a giant razor was dropped onto the fuselage of a 707. The film was a none-too-subtle attempt to show how and why the 707 had been built without the fatal flaw of the original Comet; to show why, in the company's words, the new Boeing jet would be "the safest airplane ever to be engaged in commercial air transportation."

The Boeing 707 had "rip-stop" construction, an artful term that explained the exact idea—even a gash straight into the fuselage would not cause the same sort of catastrophic decompression that had blown apart the de Havilland Comet. The interior frame of the airplane looked a bit like a Conestoga wagon, or the staves of a barrel, and it was sturdy enough to withstand the guillotine. Indeed, the tragic lessons of the Comet have been well learned. While modern jetliners have split at the panel seams and even in the case of a Boeing 737 had part of the roof sheared off as if some giant can opener in the sky had popped it open, the planes have not broken apart as the early Comets did. They have made it back to the ground.

While the major airlines had now committed to jetliners, with orders on the books for an astounding $1.1 billion of new air-craft, not everyone else was so enthusiastic. "Vast Problems of Jet Age Harass Airlines' Planners," ran the page-one headline over a 3,900-word piece in *The New York Times* one Sunday in April 1956. Indeed, the reporter had secured access to an internal Civil Aeronautics Administration document with a less-than-optimistic title: "C.A.A. Jet Age Planning—The 100 Problems."

Among them was noise: "Will the harmonics of jet noise shatter the huge picture windows that have become fashionable at modern air terminals?" Another: "What is the best machine for clearing runways of pebbles and dirt that could chew up a jet engine's insides?" A third was a concern that jet airplanes moved too fast across radar screens to be safely handled by air traffic controllers.

Moreover, many local leaders had stepped in to complain about all the impositions that would come with adapting to the new jetliners. "For fifteen years, we have been madly raising funds, lengthening runways, and enlarging airports to keep up with the growth of aviation," Atlanta mayor William B. Hartsfield had told a federal symposium on the Jet Age in early 1956. Hartsfield said airport bonds were competing with schools, highways, and other needs and that it was time to put a stop to it. Aircraft manufacturers should design new planes to fit the length of existing runways, he said, according to the *Times* article. (His call was ignored, runways were lengthened and later added, and today Atlanta's airport, named for Mayor Hartsfield and another Atlanta mayor, Maynard Jackson, is the busiest in the world.)

These problems were worked out, but the Jet Age is also interesting for the many things that could well have happened at the outset, but did not. For instance, had airline executives listened to Sir Frank Whittle, the British inventor of the jet engine, travelers between the United States and Europe would have faced not one, but two connections to reach their destinations. Sir Frank was convinced that the most economical—and safest—way to link the continents was to run dozens of shuttle flights a day between Gander, Newfoundland, and Shannon, Ireland. Under his plan, those two cities would serve as the "hubs" for flights to all other cities on their respective continents.

Since early jets were limited in range, other aviation experts were convinced that in-flight refueling was the big solution for making jet travel better. Texaco had a plan for using airborne tankers to deliver gasoline, oil, and food to domestic jets, and some diplomats envisioned a United Nations–sanctioned fleet of giant fuel-laden tankers roaming the skies, hooking up with passenger jets to give them the extra juice needed to fly nonstop from, say, Los Angeles to Athens. Even those experts couldn't resist the sexual imagery of a quickie. "The refueling process in flight would take but a few minutes," argued one, "even allowing for any trouble in finding the spot for the rendezvous of the tanker and the airliner."

That idea never caught on and, for a period of time, most of the regular public did not know exactly what the Jet Age would look like. In fact, in 1955, Trans World Airlines launched an intriguing contest promising $50,000 to the entrant who most accurately predicted what commercial aviation would be like thirty years in the future.

There were 13,000 entries, and no shortage of immensely bold visions. A man in Bombay, India, envisioned a "jetomic whizzer," a machine that would carry a thousand people and use atomic power to travel at 2,000 miles per hour. A North Dakota man said airplanes would be "fireproof, crashproof, and foolproof." Door-to-door "helitaxis" were forecast, as well as speeds of up to 25,000 miles per hour, flying hotels complete with swimming pools, and, of course, regular trips to the moon and to other planets. Some predictions were a tad timid. "T.W.A. will carry as many as 100 to 200 passengers," wrote Harwell Chatwell from Lubbock, Texas, "and they might have a movie up there, too."

In February 1986, slightly more than thirty years later, TWA called a news conference in Manhattan to announce the winner. Then a cub reporter on the metro desk of *The New York Times*, I vividly remember covering the event. The winner was Helen L. Thomas, a 1928 Radcliffe College graduate and a former editor of publications at the Research Laboratory of Electronics of the Massachusetts Institute of Technology. She said she had long forgotten about having entered the contest, but TWA officials had found her at the same address in Cambridge, Massachusetts, with which she had submitted her entry. After having reassured the now eighty-year-old Mrs. Thomas repeatedly that they were serious, they presented her with a $50,000 check.

The prizewinner had forecast with "amazing" accuracy, said TWA president Richard D. Pearson, that commercial airliners would have ranges of about 5,000 miles, cruise at 700 miles per hour or so, carry about three hundred people on long trips and be "powered by bypass jets." The victor was modest: "Having once flown in an open cockpit"—in Boston, in 1928, in a biplane, she laughingly recalled at the news conference—"I could never have predicted how luxurious air travel would become."

In the face of such wildly varying expectations and the skepticism of some public planners, Boeing was surely smart to run all its full-page magazine ads as a counterweight, touting the glory of the coming jet era. But for all the millions of dollars it spent on this advertising, the Boeing company probably had no better salesman in its force than its chief test pilot—Tex Johnston. His twin barrel rolls over Lake Washington were an unthinkable bit of barnstorming brio and when he performed them, Boeing president Bill Allen was furious. Johnston was a maverick, sure, but what he had done was both unauthorized and unthinkable. He had taken this multimillion-dollar jet airplane, still in its experimental stage, and in front of jet builders, pilots, engineers, and the heads of major airlines, he had pulled one of his old flying stunts.

Years later, in recalling his rolling of the airplane, Johnston waxed poetic about what he was trying to do.

"The most advanced, the most beautiful, the most revolutionary plane ever built, and for a few brief, wondrous moments, it lit up the skies over Lake Washington," he said. "It was a symbol of how the world was going to change, as it did change, in time and space and distance."

The day after he did it, Johnston endured a severe dressing-down from Allen and other senior Boeing officials. "What the hell were you doing yesterday?" one of them asked.

Tex held his ground. "I've always sold airplanes by demonstrating them," he said, "and I knew the audience was the IATA and all the leading engineers and scientists. There were the airplane people, rival manufacturers, everyone who meant anything in aeronautics. Never before has that quality of talent been assembled in one spot to see anyone's airplane, and probably never will be again. So I just had to do it. It was not a risk and I would never do anything to risk myself or the company's equipment." The maneuver, Tex added, was "absolutely nonhazardous, but it's very impressive."

"All right," Bill Allen said after a long moment. "You know that. Now we know that. But just don't do it anymore."

Allen never completely forgave Johnston for the stunt, nor did he ever concede that it was effective salesmanship. He spoke publicly about it only once, in May 1977, in a speech before the Seattle Historical Society. "It has taken nearly twenty-two years for me to reach the point where I can discuss the incident with a modicum of humor," Allen said. "Remember, we had $20 million and a big chunk of the company's future tied up" in the plane. "That was the only such aircraft in the world." Allen said he had been "naïve enough" to think when the first roll started that it was an accident. When Tex did it again, he was livid, but he kept it in check, as he was with guests who worked in the industry. Allen quickly realized that if he showed his anger, or followed a passing instinct to fire Johnston, *that* would become the story—not the flight itself.

Johnston elaborated on the barrel roll in a 1986 interview with Emmett Watson, a legendary columnist for both the *Seattle Post-Intelligencer* and *The Seattle Times*.

"It wasn't a risk. It was something I gave a hell of a lot of thought to," Johnston told Watson in a profile of him that appeared in the Sunday *Pacific* magazine. Or, as he explained in a later interview of his rationale: "I wouldn't jeopardize the equipment. I've perfected it all my life. These people will never forget it. They'll think it's the strongest airplane in the world."

Within the company, there was certainly controversy over what Johnston had done, but the engineers, even if not in a position to judge whether the stunt would have much Madison Avenue appeal, knew that Johnston was correct that the maneuver was not at all dangerous. "He definitely caught some hell from management," Joe Sutter, then the aerodynamics unit chief and later in his career a driving force behind the 747, said with a laugh. "But he did know exactly what he was doing. He always listened and studied very carefully when he talked with the engineers, and he would report back very carefully to us whenever he did a test [flight]. So there's this image out there of him as a hotshot, a sort of cowboy in the cockpit. That was part of him for sure, but it doesn't reflect all of him. He was a very careful pilot."

George Schairer, a key designer of the 707, who died in 2004 at the age of ninety-one, also expressed some amusement over the controversy in an interview for a company oral history, but said Johnston took his demonstration role very seriously. He thought Johnston was effectively making a declaration: "Boy, I'll show 'em how good an airplane this is!"

When Tex Johnston died in 1998 at age eighty-four, Frank Shrontz, a former Boeing chairman, credited Johnston's Lake Washington flight as "a defining moment in the success" of the 707 program. "I can't help but relate to Bill Allen's concern about betting the company," he told the *Seattle Post-Intelligencer.* "It probably was a bit of recklessness. The good news was, it worked."

It is not difficult to see both Bill Allen's and Tex Johnston's points of view. Whether it was a reckless stunt or brilliant salesmanship, Johnston's barrel roll certainly got people in the industry talking. On the very night of his dressing-down, having lived to fly another day, Johnston showed up at Allen's house in Seattle's Highlands neighborhood for a cocktail party and dinner with the aviation luminaries. Allen planned to turn and give Johnston the cold shoulder.

But before Allen could say or do anything, Eastern Air's garrulous head, Eddie Rickenbacker, the onetime Flying Ace and Medal of Honor winner, went up to Tex Johnston, grabbed his Stetson, and pulled it down over his ears.

"You slow-rolling son of a bitch!" Rickenbacker shouted joyfully at Johnston. "Why didn't you let me know you were gonna pull that? I would have been riding the jump seat!"

Rickenbacker turned to Allen. "Damn, Bill!" he said. "*That's the way to get attention with a new airplane!*"

With Pan Am's sentiment having strongly moved against the Comet, Boeing and Douglas found themselves locked in a battle for Juan Trippe's favor. Boeing had a prototype in the air and could deliver the 707 faster, but many in the industry continued to be skeptical of its ability to pull it off. Yes, Douglas was later off the mark, but with the airplanes costing upwards of $4.5 million apiece, perhaps it was better to wait a few months for the DC-8.

Characteristically, Trippe not only kept everyone in suspense, but also prodded each manufacturer for improvements—better aerodynamics, better engines, lusher interiors.

And in October 1955, Pan Am's leader was ready to drop a bombshell of an announcement: he would order both airplanes. It was the biggest airline order in history: worth a stunning $269 million, or about $2.2 billion in 2010 money. The airline would take twenty 707s, guaranteeing that it would be first among American carriers with jet service, and it would also take twenty-five DC-8s. If Trippe liked the Douglas plane better, he might sell off the 707s after a few years of service to another airline and increase the Douglas-built fleet.

In any event, the United States would finally be poised to

enter the commercial Jet Age, and Trippe milked the prose behind the event: "Breakfast in London . . . predinner swim at
Waikiki." Or, as a *New York Times* travel reporter put it, thinking of a trip in the opposite direction: "Leaving Fifth Avenue at
noon and pulling up a chair at a Parisian sidewalk café at midnight is an experience that must change anyone's estimate of the
size of his world."

The planes were "half again as big" as anything then in the
air. The first 707s could carry 125 passengers, the DC-8 had room
for 131. In a year, one plane could carry 50,000 passengers across
the Atlantic, challenging the 67,577 carried in 1954 by the mam-
moth ocean liner *United States*. Put another way, it would take
only thirty-six jetliners to fly the nearly 1.8 million passengers
Pan Am had carried in 1954 on its entire fleet of 147 propeller-
driven aircraft.

For a time, it looked as though Bill Allen's big bet might not
pay off after all. Despite the Pan Am order, United Air Lines
soon announced it had signed a contract for thirty jetliners, all of
them DC-8s. National Airlines also committed to Douglas. International airlines were paying close attention: if U.S. sentiment
was clearly tipped in favor of Douglas, the established manufacturer, they would follow suit. And once the market started trend-
ing against Boeing, it would be very hard to win it back.

The next big order would come from American Airlines,
and its president, C. R. Smith, was clearly torn. He had a long-
standing, positive relationship with Douglas, and indeed had
never bought a Boeing plane in his career. That said, he liked
the prospect that a big order could put American in a position

to follow Pan Am by only a matter of months—and be the first domestic airline to offer transcontinental jet service.

At this point, Smith lay down a huge challenge to Boeing: widen your plane by four inches, which would make the 707 one inch wider than the DC-8. That was nowhere near as easy to do as it sounded, but it would ensure that American could use the same six-abreast seating configuration as the Douglas plane in economy class, and even advertise that its passengers would enjoy wider seats (by all of a sixth of an inch) than those flying its rivals' DC-8s. The plane would need to be reengineered, the assembly machines recalibrated and in some cases retooled, a new battery of tests performed. It could slow down the entire process and add millions of dollars to the cost, and some Boeing engineers pushed back. Tell Smith to take it or leave it, they advised. Allen took it all in, and acknowledged the risks and headaches involved. But he saw bigger risks to saying no. And so he made a deal with Smith, and that small matter of inches pushed Boeing over the top. In November 1955, American announced it was now a Boeing customer. It would take thirty "Astrojet" 707s.

When the year came to a close, Douglas was still ahead, with a tally of a hundred orders to seventy-two for Boeing. But Boeing was flexible, and did a better job of listening to exactly what the customer wanted. Qantas, the scrappy and creative Australian carrier, took special modified versions; some shorter, lighter ones that could get around its network of airports in the South Pacific and a few longer-range versions that could make it to the United States West Coast with a single stopover in Hawaii.

United expressed interest in that concept of flexibility as well. Boeing's salesmen dug in for every order, and 1956 was a key turning point: by a factor of three to one, the 707 was beating out the DC-8 for orders. By the end of that year, Boeing had a lead, 141 to 123, and built on it nearly every year thereafter.

The Boeing 707 was making history in another way as well: the president of the United States wanted one, putting yet another imprimatur of prestige—and, more subtly, of safety—on the big jet. In a sort of minor version of the *Sputnik* controversy over Russian advances in space, Americans were embarrassed in the mid-1950s to see Soviet premier Khrushchev become the first head of state to be flown around in a jet airliner—the Tupolev 104. The White House put out orders for three 707s. This was the *Air Force One* model on which President Eisenhower first flew in 1959. In November 1963, when John F. Kennedy was assassinated in Dallas, Lyndon B. Johnson was sworn in as president aboard the military version of the 707, which immediately left Texas for Washington, D.C. When the final tally was added up, Boeing built slightly more than a thousand 707 jetliners—twice as many as the total Douglas deliveries of DC-8s.

For Seattle, which had at one point lost 83 percent of its Boeing-related jobs as measured against the wartime production peak, the success of both the commercial and military derivatives of the Dash-80 was a giant boost to the economy and to the region's morale. The company was constantly scouring the country for engineers, tool-and-die men, jig builders, and machinists. Most people who came to the Puget Sound region fell in love with it and wanted to stay. One story among thousands is that of Betsy and Bob Withington, a young couple who had never been out of New England when they left for Seattle shortly after their wedding in Milton, Massachusetts, in June 1941. Bob, an aerodynamicist, had a job 3,000 miles away at Boeing, where he would quickly become a vital member of the wind-tunnel research team.

"It was just beautiful, beautiful country," Betsy Withington said one day in May 2008, in the couple's home in Mercer Island, a Seattle suburb, recalling their first impressions of Seattle sixty-seven years before. "In less than two months, we'd bought a boat, we were fishing, we were skiing on the weekends. I thought the Northwest was fabulous, like a dream place to live." They never left.

For Boeing, its employees' fondness for Seattle was part of a cohesive force that gave the company a crucial advantage over rival manufacturers. In Southern California, one huge problem for Douglas, Lockheed, and some emerging aerospace companies in the postwar years was that they kept hiring away one another's talent. It is manifestly difficult to design something as complex as an airliner without a stable team of brilliant engineers and skilled workers. But that was never a problem for Boeing, and to a degree perhaps unimaginable to today's worker, the company took on an outsize, even paternalistic, role in people's lives.

The weekly *Boeing News* not only carried news of births, weddings, anniversaries, deaths, but wrote up performances by the Boeing Concert Orchestra and the Puget Sounders, a Boeing barbershop quartet. There was vivid coverage of the Boeing basketball and baseball leagues, with teams like the Stratojets, the Whizzers, the Wingdingers, and the A-Bombs. One bright Sunday morning in July 1953, four engineers from the Flight Test Group scaled Mount Rainier and planted a Boeing flag at the summit. They got the idea from photos of Mount Everest conquerors raising the Union Jack.

Boeing, all in all, was a way of life, with a notion of corporate loyalty (in both directions) that sounds absurdly quaint in today's economy. Certainly, there were labor disputes and the occasional strike, but these were worked out, and the dominant feeling in Seattle was one of immense, almost viscerally parental, pride in the company's airplanes, especially the Boeing 707. By and large, Boeing benefited from having everyone in the same place, engineers and test pilots and assembly workers freely sharing ideas about how to do better. In interviews more than fifty years after the fact, one hears over and over that Boeing's workers believed—knew—they were involved in a great enterprise. "Remember, a lot of the airlines started out saying that 'oh, Boeing's a military builder, it could not make a commercial airplane,'" Bill Cook, a top engineer, recalled with a chuckle in conversations I had with him around his ninety-fifth birthday. "And here we were, turning out a world-beating airliner, and a jetliner at that! So yes . . . sure as heck we were doing something big, and everyone knew it."

In the battle of short-range jetliners, Bill Allen's company prevailed again—more than six thousand twin-engine 737s have been built, the most of any type of jet aircraft in history, far more than the number of Douglas DC-9s. In the field of jumbo jets, the 747 outlasted both the Douglas DC-10 and the Lockheed

L-1011. Douglas eventually had to merge with a competitor, McDonnell Aircraft, and in 1996, that firm was merged into Boeing. And so the Seattle company, a three-time loser in the commercial airline market, came to dominate it.

De Havilland and the British aviation industry never fully recovered from the Comet disasters and never regained their jetliner supremacy. Even the expanded version of the jetliner, as safe to fly as its American counterparts, never made any inroads into the airliner market in the United States, although it did have some success on European routes and in Africa and South America. But in all its versions, there were barely a tenth as many de Havilland Comets produced as 707s, and the plane stopped flying long before the 707 did.

Yet there was a twist in the race to shrink the world. For while it seemed clear that the Americans had come up with the bigger, better plane that would (and did) win the long-term battle for sales, the de Havilland Comet, Mark 4, managed to score a victory as well. It was an important shot to British morale and a tribute to Britain's refusal to stay on the mat when the original Comet project proved to be such a national disaster.

On October 4, 1958, a BOAC Comet took off from London Airport headed for New York, while shortly after that another Comet started out on the opposite routing. While Pan Am had decided to set inaugural 707 service to Europe for later in the month and was building up the suspense, the British had been quiet about their own plans until more or less the day of flight. For a project that had caused so much pride and so much heartbreak, the rebirth of the Comet was a huge, happy serving of the former, and the press took note.

"British Gloat As Their Comet Wins Race to Inaugurate Transatlantic Jetliners," *The New York Times* headlined the story. *The Times* of London proclaimed, "The new age of travel begins," and the reporter said the Comet's winning flight was "a legitimate source of satisfaction for Britain." Harold Macmillan, the British prime minister, announced: "The whole nation takes pride in the fact that a British aircraft has led the world."

Plaudits came from elsewhere. In an editorial titled "Comet Comeback," *Aviation Week* magazine harked back to the era of polar adventurers when it said there was "no more traditional British characteristic than dogged determination to push on toward a goal despite any and all adversity that appears along the way.

"There is no better example of this British determination," the magazine said, "than the reappearance of the de Havilland Comet in the livery of British Overseas Airways Corp. on the world airlines after an absence of several years. The New York–London flights of the Comet 4 on Oct. 4 with just enough fare paying passengers to make a legitimate claim to being the first commercial jet operation across the Atlantic were indeed a bold stroke that provided British aviation morale a much needed boost."

And *Aeroplane*, a weekly published in London, waxed perhaps a bit much on the rhapsodic side with an editorial that proclaimed "Way Out Front," despite the fact that Pan Am's service was just a few weeks away. "No happening for many years has caught the popular imagination on both sides of the Atlantic as did the double event so brilliantly conceived and flawlessly executed by British Overseas Airways Corporation at the end of last week. To begin the regular B.O.A.C. transatlantic jet service by starting more or less simultaneously from each end of the route was a concept of genius. . . . [It] has shown that a nationalized industry can respond to enthusiastic leadership with superlative results."

BOAC took out newspaper ads praising its "first ever jet Atlantic service" and the Comet that had made the run—"the most tested airliner the world has ever known," which was perhaps a peculiar way of putting it, given the plane's tragic history, but not an inaccurate one, given the epic scope of the Hall investigation. In any event, that was past history. Now, once again, said the ad, the Comet was: "Supreme in the skies!"

Prime Minister Macmillan added a separate touching note when he sent a special message to Sir Geoffrey de Havilland: "Heartiest congratulations to you on your magnificent effort in getting the Comet 4 first off the mark in regular passenger service across the Atlantic," said the prime minister. "The resurgence of a Comet airliner is a fitting reward for faith in the future of this fine product, and the whole nation takes pride in the fact that a British aircraft has led the world into a new turbojet age."

Geoffrey de Havilland responded with an almost parental rush of emotion: "The Comet," he said, "has meant more to me than any other aeroplane we have built. It has been the most challenging, the most disheartening and finally the most technically rewarding project we have ever tackled. I am sure that it has been all of these things to the members of our enterprise."

Pan Am's big night came on October 26, when 111 passengers (instantly the largest group ever on a single airline flight) and twelve crew stepped aboard a gleaming new Boeing 707 at Idlewild Airport in New York, bound for Paris. Juan Trippe all but ignored the Comet's accomplishment, for he said this was the most important flight in history since Lindbergh's epic solo to Paris. "In one fell swoop," boasted the Emperor of the Air, "we have shrunken the earth."

Fittingly, a Boeing employee named Stephen Eastman was one of the passengers, and he made very careful notes of the entire trip, which he quickly transmitted back to his colleagues in Seattle. The Jet Age was now fully under way, as Eastman aptly recounted.

We were escorted through what seemed miles of corridors, directed at each turn by smartly dressed and ribbon-bedecked Pan Am hostesses. . . . Excitement mounted as we beheld the beautiful 707, floodlighted to best advantage from every angle, with loading lanes lined with colorful flags of all nations. . . . An hour after takeoff, many of the passengers were still running up and down aisles exclaiming over the dawn of the new era in travel. . . . Some were veterans of air travel who normally would have been settled down with ear plugs, blankets and pillows to endure the 12 or more hours of punishment from noise, vibration and buffeting in rough air at lower altitudes. . . . In no time the sky began to lighten as dawn broke swiftly ahead

of us in indescribable beauty. As the sun rose and slanted downward on the sea of clouds below, they took on the appearance
of a vast ice field tinted in all the colors of the rainbow and
extending to the far horizon.

Even as we watched this ever-changing scene, a vast break
appeared with the Atlantic seen at one edge, an immense chalk
cliff extending through the middle. There was the coast of France,
with innumerable tiny-appearing farms extending inland and
again becoming lost to view beneath the cloud cover.

The momentary glimpse of French soil seemed to have barely
fallen astern when it was announced by the skipper that our descent was about to begin. Fifteen minutes later, after plunging
into the dense layer of cloud, we drifted quietly down into the
vicinity of the airport, made a leisurely round above farms and
fields where activity ceased as all looked skyward at this new
sight and sound, and touched down at Le Bourget.

Crowds of eager French surged forward to greet us at the
end of our taxi run to the airport. It was not necessary to
understand French. "Boeing 707" was on every tongue as they
marveled at the airplane.

There were many milestone flights of the Jet Age: those of
the Comet, both triumphal and tragic, and those of the 707, including Tex Johnston's unbelievable barnstorming stunt in the
prototype, as well as this Pan Am flight from New York to Paris,
certainly iconic even if the airline had officially lost the race
to carry passengers across the Atlantic to the redesigned BOAC
Comet. The 707 became the leading plane of the Jet Age, and

until the advent of jumbo jets more than a decade later, the great majority of people who crossed the oceans did so in a Boeing 707.

Yet I like to think of one more flight that, to me anyway, illustrates in a nifty way how the human mind, not so long ago, was struggling to understand how jet travel might change our view of the world, of time and space and distance.

This was Global Airlines Flight 33, a Boeing 707 that took off uneventfully one day in 1961, headed from London Airport to New York's Idlewild Airport. In the cockpit, a team of five men guided the jet—captain, co-captain, navigator, flight engineer, and a radio man; at one point a stewardess rapped on the door and poked her head in, coyly telling the men that two stewardesses had "heavy dates" to look forward to in New York City, while she was available to any single and honorable gentleman.

Suddenly, though, the airplane hit a pocket of turbulence and started shaking all but uncontrollably. As the befuddled crew looked on, the speed dial indicated they were flying unfathomably fast—past the speed of sound, faster, way off the dial. When the captain, a man named Farver, finally got his aircraft back under control, he pointed it downward, searching for Manhattan Island. He located land but there, pausing briefly from its tree-munching to gaze menacingly up at the plane . . . was a Brontosaurus. The jet airplane had somehow traveled millions of years *back in time,* and the captain then made the bold and inevitable decision to try to fly the plane back into the turbulence, desperate to get home again to 1961. He made it as far as 1939, when an angry air controller in New York told him to quit horsing around on the radio about things nobody had ever heard of, such as Global Airlines or jet engines. Low on fuel but determined once again to fly forward in time, the desperate captain flew back toward turbulence.

"We're going to increase our speed and go back through the same sound barrier we've already done twice before," Captain Farver tells passengers over the intercom, sounding both stoic and bewildered. "I don't know if we can do it. All I ask is that you remain calm and pray."

OK. This flight never really happened. There was no Global Airlines. I couldn't see this the first time I saw the account, as a kid watching television, but the dinosaur was a cheap model. Still, the long-deceased cigarette-wielding Rod Serling and his coauthor older brother, Robert, a terrific and prolific aviation writer who typed away until the age of ninety-two, were onto something mind-bending in this classic episode they collaborated on for *The Twilight Zone*. This TV show was right up there in the pantheon of *TZ* episodes that freaked me out, along with that very young William Shatner as a recovering mental patient flying home . . . looking out the window . . . spotting a gremlin . . . oh, my God . . . ripping apart the wing! I guess I never *really* expect to have gone back or forward in time whenever I go up into the clouds and into that turbulence and come back down again in a jet airplane, but I never know for sure. And I do vividly recall Rod Serling, shaking his head over the odyssey of the mysteriously vanished transatlantic flight.

"A Global jet airliner, en route from London to New York on an uneventful afternoon in the year 1961," said Serling in his unique staccato, "but now reported overdue and missing. By now searched for on land, sea, and air by anguished human beings, fearful of what they might find. But you and I know where she is; you and I know what has happened. So if some moment, any moment, you hear the sound of jet engines flying atop the overcast skies, engines that sound searching and lost; engines that sound hungry for fuel, shoot up a flare or do something. That would be Global 33 trying to get home, from the Twilight Zone."

Epilogue

With our main characters having spent so many years in aviation—including the early, most dangerous years—and having launched such a broad array of new aircraft, it is noteworthy that all of them managed to live well past the age of eighty and die of natural causes. Bill Allen passed away in Seattle in 1985, at the age of eighty-five, of Alzheimer's disease. Tex Johnston died of the same illness, in 1998, at the age of eighty-four, in nearby Edmonds, Washington. He was preceded in death by his wife, DeLores, to whom—despite his incorrigibly flirtatious ways—he was happily married for sixty years.

Sir Geoffrey de Havilland, having lost two of his sons in the prime of their youth in accidents aboard his company's planes, died in 1965 at the age of eighty-two, of a cerebral hemorrhage. The man who in some ways became a surrogate son to him, John "Cat's Eyes" Cunningham, the de Havilland chief test pilot for all of the Comet's test flights, survived numerous aerial battles in World War II and registered at least twenty kills. Despite the Comet's tragic legacy, Cunningham himself never suffered so much as a scratch aboard the airliner. He died in his sleep at a nursing home in 2002, days before his eighty-fifth birthday. And Sir Arnold Hall, the chief investigator of the Comet disasters, went on to have a long career in aviation. He served as the head of Hawker Siddeley—the concern that bought up the de Havilland company after the firm staggered under the weight of the Comet's costs—and died at age eighty-four in 2000.

For the de Havilland Comet, the victory over the 707 in the cross-Atlantic race was, of course, Pyrrhic. The Comets never came close to regaining their world-beating role, and in fact, BOAC soon stopped flying them on transatlantic runs, in favor of the bigger 707. The Comet ceased production in 1964, with a total of 112 built over a fifteen-year span, seventy-six of them the largest model, the Comet 4. While the plane never made its mark in the transoceanic field and no American carrier ever bought one, it did see years of successful service with nearly two dozen carriers throughout Europe, Africa, Asia, South America, Mexico, and Canada. The last airline to use it was Dan-Air, a London-based intra-European carrier that stopped Comet service in 1980. The last flight on the Comet was in 1997, a Comet 4C owned by the British government. Although there are a handful of Comet airplanes at British airfields, including the de Havilland Aircraft Heritage Centre in Hatfield, and the Seattle-based Museum of Flight is currently restoring a Comet 4 for display, none of these remaining planes are flightworthy.

The Boeing 707 continues to fly today as a cargo carrier in parts of Africa and South America, but the last known passenger carrier, Saha Airlines of Iran, ceased scheduled flights in 2009.

All told, Boeing built 1,010 of the 707s for civilian use, nearly double the total number of DC-8s produced by rival Douglas, which Boeing eventually acquired. Hundreds more of the military derivatives of the Dash-80, the KC-135, are still in use by the U.S. Air Force today and in good enough shape, the Pentagon says, that some could still be flying in 2040. Though it was the third jet airliner built, the fifth to fly, and the runner-up in the 1958 transatlantic race, the Seven Oh Seven was the clear winner in the most important aspect of the jetliner competition, for it was the plane that both defined and dominated the Jet Age.

SOURCES AND ACKNOWLEDGMENTS

A good friend of mine likes to say that people don't care how the milk gets to the porch, they just want the milk. To which I can only add the observation that people no longer seem to want their milk (or, alas, their daily newspaper) even delivered to the porch. So, if you just want the milk, by all means skip this. But if you're interested, as many readers are, in where the idea for this book came from and how I put together the research, then please take a seat on the porch.

Like a lot of books, this one started out as something different. I was looking to do a biography of Bill Boeing, who remains a fascinating character to me, but something about the story didn't quite work. As I explain in this book, Boeing's tiny float-plane company on Lake Union in Seattle became the spearhead behind what are today three huge international corporations: the Boeing Company, United Air Lines, and United Technologies. Yet Boeing was irate over the 1934 actions by President Franklin D. Roosevelt and the U.S. Congress that split his empire into three—an airplane company, an airline, and an engine manufacturer—and so he quit all three industries in disgust. He enjoyed himself, developing property and raising thoroughbred horses, and when he died aboard his yacht twenty-two years later, three days before he would have turned seventy-five, he was still a very wealthy man. Curiously, though, he owned not one share of Boeing stock, and the man with the iconic name was simply not a player in two decades' worth of amazing developments in air travel, including the invention of the jet engine and the jet airliner.

The man who did grab hold of my imagination, Bill Allen, was as influential as any other single figure in the development of the modern jet airliner. He took over a company worth $13.8 million in 1945, and left the presidency twenty-five years later, when it was worth $3.3 billion. I became particularly interested in the series of canny legal, financial, and engineering moves that allowed the company to develop hugely successful military and commercial airplanes out of one remarkable prototype—the Dash-80, the airplane that test pilot Tex Johnston so memorably "barrel-rolled" over Seattle's Lake Washington in the summer of 1955. Bill Allen was smart enough to pull off the first two moves, and perhaps even smarter to give his team of engineers his complete trust and faith to pull off the third.

At the same time, I quickly began to see that Boeing and other U.S. manufacturers had certainly been spurred to act by a pioneering, tragically doomed airplane across the Pond, the British de Havilland Comet. The Comet was years ahead of any other jet airliner—too many years ahead, it turned out. I found myself agreeing with a book published in Great Britain in 1955, *The Comet Riddle*, which stated simply, boldly, and, I think, quite truthfully: "The Comet jet airliner was the most spectacular aircraft ever built. Its failure was equally spectacular."

It was hard not to see the two airplanes as apt metaphors for the nations that produced them, and perhaps as an American I was especially tempted by the facile narrative. The Comet—what a tragically appropriate name—was the product of a war-ravaged, fading empire, on its way to becoming (temporarily) the economic Sick Man of Europe, while the sleekly named 707 was a perfect symbol for a postwar America, ascendant, prosperous, confident, and successful. All true, to a degree, but all too simplistic, I concluded. For one thing, it was the supposedly hidebound British who decided to push into the future of jet travel, while American manufacturers and airlines traded all the reasons and shuffled through the paperwork not to do it.

Even as I had to repeatedly remind myself that I might view the situation very differently had a loved one of mine died aboard a de Havilland Comet, I developed a tremendous admiration for the British builders and engineers who pushed the envelope and came up with a creation that amazed the world. I was most curious about Sir Geoffrey de Havilland: What drove a man who had already lost two of his three sons in crashes in his own airplanes to keep building airplanes? I also developed an admiration for the de Havilland company's chief test pilot, John Cunningham: no barrel-rolling showman he, but as consummate an aviator as his brash, flamboyant American counterpart at Boeing, Tex Johnston. And, I decided, there was certainly one more man who deserved to be a character in the book: Sir Arnold Hall, the brilliant aeronautics professor tasked with answering the Comet riddle.

Jet Age is by no means the first or last book about either of these aircraft, although I believe it is the first that focuses on both of them as their creators raced to "shrink the world" by being first to carry passengers in jet service across either of the world's great oceans. Nor is it the first or last book about the so-called Golden Age of air travel, and later in this section, bibliography style, I list the publications that I consulted before telling this story. These include a raft of great books about the history of the Boeing company; a lesser number of equally compelling accounts about the now defunct de Havilland company; autobiographies of a few of my main characters, including Sir Geoffrey de Havilland and Tex Johnston; and a few books that were so interesting and entertaining I would like to highlight them now for readers who may wish to know more about their topics. I have necessarily telescoped these last, since they are not at the heart of my own book; they include *Femininity in Flight*, Kathleen M. Barry's marvelous history of flight attendants; Jay Spenser's *The Airplane: How Ideas Gave Us Wings*, whose subtitle explains precisely what his book is about; Daniel L. Rust's *Flying Across America*, a beautifully illustrated, lyrical guide to the history of the airline passenger experience; *The Sporty Game*, John Newhouse's classic about the high-risk commercial airliner business in the jumbo-jet era; and two excellent books about Juan Trippe, the "Emperor of the Air": *An American Saga: Juan Trippe and His Pan Am Empire*, by Robert Daley, and *The Chosen Instrument: Pan Am, Juan Trippe, the Rise and Fall of an American Entrepreneur*, by Marilyn Bender and Selig Altschul.

When asked about the book while I was researching, I tended to say it was about the race to build the first jet airliner, which was—is—fine as far as it goes. But of course, it turns out to be a little more complicated than that. There is no question about who built the first jetliner. The narrative really pits the British, racing to find and fix the flaw in their pioneering jetliner, against the American upstarts, who wound up with what is sometimes called in business terms the "second-mover advantage." In essence, a second mover gets the benefit of having some idea of where the first mover failed. The Comet failures took more than a hundred lives.

With this general narrative in mind, I turned to a number of sources for help, several right here in my adopted hometown. The Seattle Public Library has an extraordinary collection of material in the Maffei Family Aviation Room of the central library building. Not so surprising that there would be a huge set of books, magazines, newspaper clippings, brochures, lectures, and other information about aviation in Jet City, in the region where Boeing has built every major jet airliner from the 707 Jet Stratoliner to the 787 Dreamliner. What I did not expect was for there to be so much great source material about British aviation, including official accounts of the Comet inquiry and several books about the Comet program and the history of the de Havilland company. I am very grateful to both the former and the current executive directors of the library's Washington Center for the Book, Nancy Pearl and Chris Higashi, for turning me on to this collection. (Nancy has gone on to be the author of the popular Book Lust series. She is, in my opinion anyway, completely deserving of her status as the second-best-selling action figure of all time at the Archie McPhee novelty company: indeed, the Pearl librarian action figure, with its automatic index-finger-to-mouth *shush*ing feature, outsells Leonardo, Einstein, Freud, and Houdini, and currently runs second in sales only to Jesus Christ. A testament to Seattle's bookish soul.)

My next two stops were also local. One was the Boeing Historical Archives, whose director, Michael Lombardi, has been extraordinarily helpful in unearthing a trove of oral history interviews, telephone transcripts, diaries, news clippings, photographs, engineering drawings, and other material, all topped off by his securing of the infamous "guillotine film" and a reel-to-reel projector to show it. I am immensely grateful. The other was Seattle's awesome Museum of Flight, one more treasure trove of aviation material from around the world. A big thank you to Janice Baker, the director of the museum's archives, for opening them to me; and to Amy Heidrick, the photo archivist, for producing boxes of photographs for me to peruse and select for the book. The museum's 2008 *Style in the Aisle* exhibit, about flight attendants, was terrific, and I'll never forget the

Saturday event in which dozens of ex-stewardesses (proud to call themselves that, thank you very much) showed up in their uniforms, some dating back to the 1940s, for a panel discussion about their working lives in the sky. In Everett, Washington, north of Seattle, Jim Goodall regaled me with tales and tours of the meticulous restoration project in progress there, under the museum's auspices, of a de Havilland Comet Mark 4.

Also, locally, countless Boeing people shared their stories with me. I couldn't possibly list them all, so I would simply like to highlight a few. One of the best and most pleasurable days of my own reporting life was spent with a collection of Boeing engineers and pilots who gathered one day in March 2008 at the home of Betsy and Bob Withington in Mercer Island, Washington, to tell me as much as they could about their own 707-related work and about the Boeing company, Bill Allen, and Tex Johnston. They were all young men back then, but not so young at the time of our interview, and I appreciate the considerable effort each of them made to be there. So, thank you, Bill Cook, Guy Townsend, Brien Wygle, and Bob Withington. I apologize to these and all the other engineers I've interviewed for the ways in which my technological explanations for the lay reader inevitably boil down the intricacies of their work. I have been fascinated by airplanes my whole life and have spent much time in the last few years studying the mechanics of jet propulsion. I think I can now explain it, but I still don't quite believe it: I confess that I'm still basically amazed every time I see a humpbacked 747 lumber down the runway, gather speed, and actually get off the ground. And a special thank you to Betsy Withington, whose descriptions of moving from her native Massachusetts to Washington state in the 1940s (paralleling my own somewhat more circuitous migration a half-century later) set off a lightbulb in my head about one reason Boeing did so well: once it got the talent here, nobody wanted to leave.

Joe Sutter, the legendary 747 designer and the chief aerodynamicist for the 707, offered me many vivid observations and memories. I'm grateful to Bill Boeing, Jr., the son of the company founder, for help with some family history. My uncle-in-law Gerald Herman, a Boeing man, was and remains a source of endlessly entertaining stories about flight in general and Boeing in particular, and he was an important inspiration to me in taking on this book. Richard Eger provided me with an unexpected boost at a perfect time by unearthing a trove of Royal Air Force material about the Allied encounter with the Messerschmitt Me 262. The late Walt Crowley, the founding director and guiding spirit of Seattle's historylink.org, was helpful with some early Blue Moon (ale)–centric discussions and his wisdom.

In England, I was fortunate in having tremendous hosts for several days of de Havilland–related research, most especially at the de Havilland Aircraft Heritage Centre in Hertfordshire, where volunteers have committed themselves, in a true labor of love, to restore old airplanes carrying the famous DH brand. Thank you to John Tidmarsh for showing me around, and here's hoping that the Centre's efforts will ultimately be rewarded with the funds and interest to enable it to restore the now forlorn old fuselage of an Air France Comet 1-A on its grounds. Similarly, I felt a tug of mixed feelings when I landed at Bruntingthorpe

one June day in 2008 to see the last Comet ever to fly, the Canopus; the grand project by the National Air Pageant to make her
flightworthy had to be abandoned several years ago for lack of
funds. Every Briton should be proud of the pioneering jet Comet.
This plane, even if it never flies again, deserves a proper home
in a museum, with a gleaming retro livery. That said, it was a
tremendous thrill for me to see the Canopus, and I am deeply
grateful to Eamonn Molloy for flying me over from Oxford on
that memorable early-summer day. Jim Davies and Paul Jarvis,
of the British Airways Heritage Centre, were very helpful with
BOAC research and Comet photographs. I am also grateful to
Marc Ventresca for hospitality in Oxford, and, in London, for a
similar welcome from Miguel and Marina Sánchez, Sarah Lyall
and Robert McCrum, and ace pilot Kim Murphy.

In addition to the reporting and interviews listed above, and
with the help of Seattle librarians and ever more powerful search
software, I read through several years' worth of articles and ad-
vertisements from the following newspapers: *The New York
Times*, *The Washington Post*, the *Los Angeles Times*, *The Wall Street
Journal*, *The Seattle Times*, the *Seattle Post-Intelligencer*, *The
Times* of London, and *The Manchester Guardian*. I read articles
from *Time*, *Life*, *Newsweek*, *Flight*, and *Aviation Week*, as well as
numerous publications of several of the aircraft manufacturers and airlines mentioned in *Jet Age*.

I also read and took notes from the following, which are
listed alphabetically by author, not by any personal preference of
mine or suggestion of any order of their importance in shaping
this book. I hope that no author will feel that I have misinter-

preted or given overly short shrift to his or her work, and while I have done my best to double- and triple-check every fact and quotation in my book, I apologize and accept responsibility for any errors.

Allen, Oliver E. *Th Airline Builders*. Chicago: Time-Life Books, 1981.

Angelucci, Enzo. *Airplanes: From the Dawn of Flight to the Present Day*. New York: McGraw-Hill, 1973.

Bain, Gordon. *De Havilland: A Pictorial Tribute*. London: Airlife, 1992.

Barry, Kathleen M. *Femininity in Flight: A History of Flight Attendants*. Durham, NC, and London: Duke University Press, 2007.

Bauer, Eugene E. *Boeing: The First Century*. Enumclaw, WA: TABA, 2000.

Bauer, Eugene E. *Boeing in Peace and War*. Enumclaw, WA: TABA, 1991.

Bender, Marilyn, and Selig Altschul. *The Chosen Instrument: Pan Am, Juan Trippe, the Rise and Fall of an American Entrepreneur*. New York: Simon & Schuster, 1982.

Berg, A. Scott. *Lindbergh*. New York: G. P. Putnam's Sons, 1998.

Biddle, Wayne. *Barons of the Sky*. New York: Simon & Schuster, 1991.

Bilstein, Roger E. "Air Travel and the Traveling Public: The American Experience, 1920–1970." In William F. Trimble, *From Airships to Airbus: The History of Civil and Commercial Aviation*, vol. 2. Washington, DC: Smithsonian Institution Press, 1992.

SOURCES AND ACKNOWLEDGMENTS

Bilstein, Roger E. *Flight in America: From the Wrights to the Astronauts*, rev. ed. Baltimore: The Johns Hopkins University Press, 1994.

Boeing Company. "William Allen: A Personal Portrait" (pamphlet). Seattle: The Boeing Company, n.d.

Boyne, Walter J., and Donald S. Lopez, eds. *The Jet Age: Forty Years of Jet Aviation*. Washington, DC: Smithsonian Institution Press, 1979.

Bright, Charles D. *The Jet Makers: The Aerospace Industry from 1945 to 1972*. Lawrence: The Regents Press of Kansas, 1978.

Brock, Horace, and Jason Aronson. *Flying the Oceans: A Pilot's Story of Pan Am*. New York: Jason Aronson, 1978.

Brooks, Peter W. *The Modern Airliner: Its Origin and Development*. London: Putnam, 1961.

Caidin, Martin. *Boeing 707*. New York: Ballantine, 1959.

Collins, Gail. *When Everything Changed: The Amazing Journey of American Women From 1960 to the Present*. New York: Little, Brown, 2009.

Cook, William H., with Tandy Y. Cook. *The Road to the 707: The Inside Story of Designing the 707*. Bellevue, WA: TYC, 1991.

D'Antonio, Michael. *A Ball, a Dog, and a Monkey: 1957, the Space Race Begins*. New York: Simon & Schuster, 2007.

Daley, Robert. *An American Saga: Juan Trippe and His Pan Am Empire*. New York: Random House, 1980.

Darling, Kev. *De Havilland Comet*. North Branch, MN: Specialty Press, 2001.

Darling, Kev. *De Havilland Comet*. Ramsbury, England: The Crowood Press, 2005.

Davies, R. E. G. *Airlines of the United States Since 1914*. Washington, DC: Smithsonian Institution Press, 1982.

Davies, R. E. G. *Pan Am: An Airline and Its Aircraft*. New York: Crown, 1987.

Davies, R. E. G., and Philip J. Birtles. *De Havilland Comet: The World's First Jet Airliner*. McLean, VA: Paladwr Press, 1999.

de Havilland, Sir Geoffrey. *Sky Fever: The Autobiography of Sir Geoffrey de Havilland*. London: Hamish Hamitton, 1961.

Dienel, Hans-Liudger, and Lyth, Peter, eds. *Flying the Flag: European Commercial Air Transport Since 1945*. New York: St. Martin's Press, 1998.

English, Dave. *Slipping the Surly Bonds: Great Quotations on Flight*. New York: McGraw-Hill, 1998.

Ferguson, Niall. *Empire: The Rise and Demise of the British World Order and the Lessons for Global Power*. London: Allen Lane, 2002.

Francillon, René J. *Boeing 707: Pioneer Jetliner*. Osceola, WI: MBI, 1999.

Gandt, Robert L. *Skygods: The Fall of Pan Am*. New York: William Morrow, 1995.

Goldman, Eric F. *The Crucial Decade—and After: America, 1945–1960*. New York: Vintage, 1960.

Grant, R. G. *Flight: 100 Years of Aviation: The Complete History*. New York: DK Publishing, in association with the National Air and Space Museum, Smithsonian Institution, 2002.

Gunston, Bill. *The Jet Age*. London: Arthur Barker, 1971.

Halaby, Najeeb E. *Crosswinds: An Airman's Memoir*. New York: Doubleday, 1978.

Halberstam, David. *The Fifties*. New York: Fawcett/Random House, 1993.

Hallion, Richard P. *Taking Flight: Inventing the Aerial Age from Antiquity Through the First World War*. Oxford and New York: Oxford University Press, 2003.

Heppenheimer, T. A. *Turbulent Skies: The History of Commercial Aviation*. New York: John Wiley & Sons, 1995.

Hertog, Susan. *Anne Morrow Lindbergh: Her Life*. New York: Anchor, 2000.

Hess, William N., and Kenn C. Rust. "The German Jets and the U.S. Army Air Force." *American Aviation Historical Society Journal* 8 (Fall 1963), pp. 155–162.

Hewat, Timothy, and W. A. Waterton. *The Comet Riddle*. London: Frederick Muller, 1955.

Jackson, A. J. *De Havilland Aircraft Since 1915*. London: Putnam, 1962.

Johnston, A. M. "Tex," with Charles Barton. *Tex Johnston: Jet-Age Test Pilot*. Washington, DC, and London: Smithsonian Institution Press, 1991.

Jones, Glyn. *The Jet Pioneers: The Birth of Jet-Powered Flight*. London: Methuen, 1989.

Josephson, Matthew. *Empire of the Air: Juan Trippe and the Struggle for World Airways*. New York: Harcourt, Brace, 1944.

Kaplan, Fred. *1959: The Year Everything Changed*. Hoboken, NJ: John Wiley & Sons, 2010.

Kemp, Kenny: *Flight of the Titans: Boeing, Airbus and the Battle for the Future of Air Travel*. London: Virgin, 2006.

Lipsner, Benjamin B., and Leonard Finley Hilts. *The Airmail: Jennies to Jets*. Chicago: Wilcox and Follett, 1951.

Lynn, Matthew. *Birds of Prey: Boeing vs. Airbus: A Battle for the Skies*. New York: Four Walls Eight Windows, 1998.

Mansfield, Harold. *Vision: A Saga of the Sky: The Story of Boeing*. New York: Duell, Sloan and Pearce, 1956.

Markham, Beryl. *West with the Night*. New York: North Point Press, 1983 (orig. pub. 1942).

McLaughlin, Helen E. *Footsteps in the Sky: An Informal Review of U.S. Airlines Inflight Service, 1920–Present*. Denver: State of the Art, 1994.

Mead, Walter Russell. *God and Gold: Britain, America, and the Making of the Modern World*. New York: Random House, 2007.

Mondey, David, and Michael J. H. Taylor, eds. *Milestones of Flight*. London: Jane's, 1983.

Munson, Kenneth. *Pictorial History of BOAC and Imperial Airways*. Skepperton, England: Ian Allen, 1970.

Nelson, Gerald B. *Seattle: The Life and Times of an American City*. New York: Alfred A. Knopf, 1977.

Newhouse, John. *Boeing Versus Airbus: The Inside Story of the Greatest International Competition in Business*. New York: Alfred A. Knopf, 2007.

Newhouse, John. *The Sporty Game: The High-Risk Competitive Business of Making and Selling Commercial Airliners*. New York: Alfred A. Knopf, 1982.

Nye, David E. *American Technological Sublime*. Cambridge, MA: The MIT Press, 1996.

Ott, James, and Aram Gesar. *Jets: Airliners of the Golden Age*. Shrewsbury, England: Airlife, 1993; repr. 1996.

Ott, James, and Raymond E. Neidl. *Airline Odyssey: The Airline Industry's Turbulent Flight into the Future*. New York: McGraw-Hill, 1995.

Penrose, Harold. *Wings Across the World: An Illustrated History of British Airways*. London: Cassell, 1980.

Petroski, Henry. *To Engineer Is Human: The Role of Failure in Successful Design*. New York: St. Martin's Press, 1985.

Rae, John B. *Climb to Greatness: The American Aircraft Industry, 1920–1960*. Cambridge, MA: The MIT Press, 1968.

Ramsden, Mike. "John Cunningham: Night Fighter Ace and Comet Test Pilot: 1917–2002" (pamphlet). London Colney, England: de Havilland Aircraft Heritage Centre, n.d.

Redding, Robert, and Bill Yenne. *Boeing: Planemaker to the World*. Greenwich, CT: Bison/Crescent, 1983.

Rodgers, Eugene. *Flying High: The Story of Boeing and the Rise of the Jetliner Industry*. New York: Atlantic Monthly Press, 1996.

Rust, Daniel L. *Flying Across America: The Airline Passenger Experience*. Norman: University of Oklahoma Press, 2009.

Saint-Exupéry, Antoine de. *Wind, Sand and Stars*. Trans. Lewis Galantière. New York: Harcourt Brace Jovanovich, 1967 (orig. pub. 1939).

Sampson, Anthony. *Empires of the Sky: The Politics, Contests and Cartels of World Airlines*. New York: Random House, 1984.

Schwartz, Rosalie. *Flying Down to Rio: Hollywood, Tourists, and

Yankee Clippers. College Station: Texas A&M University Press, 2004.

Sell, T. M. *Wings of Power: Boeing and the Politics of Growth in the Northwest*. Seattle: University of Washington Press, 2001.

Serling, Robert J. *Legend & Legacy: The Story of Boeing and Its People*. New York: St. Martin's Press, 1992.

Shamburger, Page. *Tracks Across the Sky*. New York: J. B. Lippincott, 1964.

Sharp, C. Martin. *D.H.: A History of de Havilland*. Shrewsbury, England: Airlife, 1982.

Simonson, Gene Roger, ed. *The History of the American Aircraft Industry: An Anthology*. Cambridge, MA: The MIT Press, 1968.

Smith, Henry Ladd. *Airways: The History of Commercial Aviation in the United States*. New York: Russell & Russell, 1965.

Solberg, Carl. *Conquest of the Skies: A History of Commercial Aviation in America*. Boston and Toronto: Little, Brown, 1979.

Spenser, Jay. *The Airplane: How Ideas Gave Us Wings*. Washington, DC: Smithsonian Books, in association with HarperCollins, 2008.

Spitz, Bob. *The Beatles: The Biography*. New York: Back Bay/Little, Brown, 2005.

Steele, Gordon John. *A Thread Across the Ocean: The Heroic Story of the Transatlantic Cable*. New York: Walker, 2002.

Stein, Elissa. *Stewardess: Come Fly with Me!* San Francisco: Chronicle, 2006.

Sutter, Joe, with Jay Spenser. *747: Creating the Jumbo Jet and Other Adventures from a Life in Aviation*. Washington, DC: Smithsonian Books, in association with HarperCollins, 2006.

Szurovy, Geva. *The Art of the Airways*. Saint Paul: Zenith Press, 2002.

Taylor, Frank J. *High Horizons: Daredevil Flying Postmen to Modern Magic Carpet—The United Air Lines Story*. New York: McGraw-Hill, 1964.

Thomas, Sir Miles. *Out on a Wing: An Autobiography*. London: Michael Joseph, 1964.

Van Vleck, Jenifer L. "The 'Logic of the Air': Aviation and the Globalism of the 'American Century.'" *New Global Studies* 1, no. 1 (2007), 1–37.

Wolfe, Tom. *The Right Stuff*. New York: Farrar, Straus & Giroux, 1979.

Each of the quotations and factual details in this book comes from one of the sources listed above and, where possible, in such matters as a public news briefing or hearing, from multiple sources. In cases in which a quotation describes someone's thinking at any given moment of time, the source is either an interview with or a public statement by that person, or a quotation taken from his autobiography, generally sourced as such in the text of the book. Unfortunately, to paraphrase Tex Johnston, my flight plan in life never crossed with his, but I do believe he would forgive me for taking some of his prodigious power of memory with a grain of salt. I am technically on solid ground by using his account of events and sourcing them accordingly, but I think it quite possible that a few details of Tex's vivid stories were flights of fancy. I mean no disrespect—in fact, the opposite—by saying that in addition to being a test pilot extraordinaire, Tex was clearly a masterly storyteller.

In a twenty-five-year newspaper career, I was blessed with a number of editors who made me a better reporter and writer and who ultimately gave me the encouragement (I think I know now why "courage" is part of that word) to take on a book. I am especially grateful to Soma Golden, Joe Lelyveld, Dean Baquet, Katy Roberts, Paul Fishleder, Scott Kraft, and Kelly Scott. John Carroll went out of his way to send me the most graceful notes of support at a difficult time, and I will never forget such a simple but profound kindness. Finally, Bob McFadden was perhaps the scariest rewrite man this cub reporter ever had to work for—"How many steps were there in the stairs? What color was the wallpaper? Call me back when you've done some real reporting!"—but I learned more from him about the art of reporting than from any other single person I worked for or with at *The New York Times* or the *Los Angeles Times*.

David McCormick is a terrific agent, and I'm grateful that he expressed an interest in my work long before I even came up with the book proposal, which he in turn sharpened into something much better. Though I wound up with a different publisher, Tom Mayer, an editor at W. W. Norton, showed an early and enthusiastic interest in the concept and gave me several ideas, for which I extend my thanks.

The editor and publisher who did take me on, Megan Newman, at Avery, has my continuing deep gratitude, as well as my apologies for all the extra care and feeding this novice author required of her. Also at Avery, I am most grateful to Jeff Galas for the early guidance in shaping the book, and to Miriam Rich for sticking with me to the end.

I come now to a last round of personal thanks, a part that I now see why many authors dread, for fear of inevitably leaving someone out. Apologies if I do. Thank you to those who endured both the early draft and the final sweats: Scott McCartney, Tim Egan, Tim Golden, Bill McKibben, Sue Halpern, Peter Howe, Holly LeCraw Howe, and Jim Fallows, with an extra thanks to Scott and Jim for taking me flying, and an extra apology to Bill for expending all the carbon.

Others helped me in countless ways with acts of love and/or friendship: Joni Balter, Lisa Belkin, Thaddeus Herrick and Linda Ebaugh, Barb and Dave Boardman, Lynn Marshall, Tomas Alex Tizon, Betsy Kolbert and John Kleiner, Kevin Sack, Annie Finnigan, Jesse Katz, Patricia Ortega, Maureen Balleza, Tim Fleck, Karen Blumenthal, Kim and David Sterling, Mimi Swartz and John Wilburn, Betsy and Josh Breier, Patty Stonesifer and Michael Kinsley, Anne and Shirish Mulherkar, Lisa and Tom Cohen, Kathy Weber, Magna DoCanto, Lisa and Joel Benenson, Joel Connelly, Knute Berger, Maria Limon, John Marshall, George Divoky, Kevin Hamilton, Tunie Hamlen, Rick Simonson, Sherry Prowda, Kip Robinson, Steve Melson, Joe Swayze,

Evelyn Iritani and Roger Ainsley, Maggie and Trevor Neilson, Andrew and Joy Dodds, John Sessions, Kenan Block, Kim and Jeff Seely, Margaret Lane and Steven Caplow, Jessica Kowal and Blaine Harden, Liz Swift, Harrison Miller, Michael Knoll, Cary Melton and Mike Seely, Rich Read, Stephanie Richardson, Wendy Jane Fay, Annie Hall Levine, and P. T. McGleughlin. Special hugs to Mary Porter and Mary Spencer.

In our little village of Magnolia, where our kids went to school and played on the recreational sports teams, we are blessed with so many good friends and good times, the special ones that blossom from PTA meetings and hours spent coaching, standing on rainy sidelines, or sitting in crowded gyms. Thank you, Gab, Doc John, Lou, Linda H. (both of you), Leanne, Randy, Karin, Seanna, Paul, Suzanne, Chris, Robyn, George Clooney (I mean Vee), Bill Barks, Tami, Jill, Sara, Bill, Sheri, Brian, Leslie, Marie, and David Z. Lindsay, Dana, and Norm, truly wonderful Magnolians all, live on in spirit here. Special thanks to Tim "The Ice Man" Murphy for the golf and the Boston humor, and to Luann for the Discovery Park walks.

I am grateful most of all to my family. I am lucky to have parents-in-law I adore, Jim and Mary, and the same goes for my various other in-laws and the Outlaws; you know who you are. Sylvia Burleigh Sánchez, my late mother's sister and best friend, is a constant source of love and support, as was her late husband, my uncle Gil. I lean on my brothers perpetually for love, wisdom, and all the e-mail banter—thanks, Harry, John, and P.J. I miss my sister, Sylvia, and my parents, Barbara and Murray, and wish they could have been around to see the kid—who collected real airline timetables and created imaginary ones—actually generate a book about the jets. My three children, Gordie, Alice, and Johnny, are a source of great joy, love, and support; no father could ask for better. The deepest part of my heart belongs to Lisa: supporting this book is one of a million ways she shows her love.

Sam Howe Verhovek
Seattle, 2010

INDEX

Page numbers in italics indicate illustrations.

INDEX

INDEX

INDEX